本书惠承乐俊民严赛虹基金会赞助出版

The publication of this bilingual anthology is sponsored by
Iris and Junming Le Foundation

美国华语诗人双语作品选

Selected Works of American Chinese Poets
A Bilingual Anthology

严力 邱辛晔 选编

Selected and Edited by Yan Li Qiu Xinye

梅丹理 英文翻译

Translated by Denis Mair

易文出版社
I Wing Press, New York

Selected Works of American Chinese Poets A Bilingual Anthology

Selected and Edited by Yan Li   Qiu Xinye

Translated by Denis Mair

Published by I Wing Press, New York
iwingpress@gmail.com
July 2024, First Edition, First Printing
ISBN：   978-1-961768-02-4

美国华语诗人双语作品选

严力   邱辛晔   选编

梅丹理   英文翻译

封面作品：岛　子（蓝色晚餐，2015 年）
装帧设计：王昌华
出 版 人：冰　寒

出　　版：易文出版社·纽约
版　次：   2024 年 7 月第一版，第一次印刷
字　数：   30 千字
定　价： $25.00

Copyright © 2024 by I Wing Press, all rights reserved.
No part of this book may be reproduced in any form or by any electronic
or mechanical means including information storage and retrieval systems,
without permission in writing from the publisher. The only exception is
by a reviewer, who may quote short excerpts in review.

作品内容受国际知识产权公约保护，版权所有，侵权必究

序　言

　　中国现代诗从诞生起就处于尴尬的处境中，预示其未来百年发展的种种波折，以及面对的一轮接一轮挑战。现代诗是中国五四新文化运动、五四新文学的一个部分，它写下第一行诗句时，就以挑战和否定传统诗歌的历史、文法、语言为使命；它的尝试者和推动者，大多有着激进思想，怀着把诗行作为利剑与犁头的理想主义，即使鲁莽也不以为意；新诗的作者同时大口呼吸西方文学的气息，或通过阅读原著，或以翻译为媒介——后者尤其肌肉发达，影响力巨大，乃至早期中国现代诗歌，把翻译体的西方诗歌，作为纯粹的营养液，一口口吞下，再创造出汉语的白话文体诗歌，乃至从骨髓到外衣，是既慕"洋派"又务"通俗"的双体。了解中国现代文学历史的读者和诗人，对此当不陌生。自然，我们并非说中国现代诗歌全然是单调和单薄的。"尝试"到"创造"的轨道边上，还有"湖畔"和"象征"；三十和四十年代，"现代"和"七月""九叶"鼎立，颇为壮观。期间，最为明显的就是西方诗歌的影响，现代汉语诗的范式，不出其右。五十年代后，中国大陆诗歌尚以现实主义，堪与论者稀，而台湾现代诗则流派纷呈，诗人辈出，现代汉语也逐渐成熟，能担负起诗人的情怀了。这期间白话文洗去了多少翻译体的尴尬，重新吸取了多少古典汉语的精髓，诗人比读者更清楚。当中国大陆再次展示新诗的力道，则是二十多年以后了：以意象为特征的朦胧诗，从"今天"到"一行"，异军突起，标志着中国大陆现代诗歌从早期的蹒跚、跌撞中凤凰涅槃，不让对岸新诗之日日新。

1987 年在纽约创立的《一行》，是出生于海外而开创汉语诗歌本体风格、复兴诗歌精神的实践。由于在海外的独特位置，自由出版的环境，海内外诗人得以各擅其长，杂志风格兼容多样，千百位诗人由此平台脱颖而出，对今后数十年现代诗歌各种"流派""主义"，以及各种民刊，影响甚巨。正是在这个脉络中，"一行"提倡的对人类普遍价值的关注、对人类种种行为的反思，承担当代人对当代事件记录的责任，值得延续和传承。2019 年，"一行"在停刊十多年后复刊，以《纽约一行》为刊名。复刊后的艺文杂志，出版纸本季刊，已完成了 14 期，于海内外诗文界流布、图书馆收藏；同时出版双周电子刊，已近百期，上刊诗人数以百计。和当年《一行》之作者大多数来自中国大陆的情况略微不同的是：1987 年到 2000 年间，这本杂志是大陆诗人可以仰赖的不多的民刊，而且身居海外，享有较高出版和创作的自由度；如今的《纽约一行》，虽然大陆诗人依旧踊跃，诗人中亦不乏居住在美国、欧洲和世界各地的华裔诗人，他们用汉语写诗，把母语作为精神的故乡、独立意识的依托。他们之中的大多数不仅懂得而且有相当程度的英文能力。一百多年前中国白话文运动中诞生的现代诗，至此似乎来了一个反转：华裔诗人因其居处，因其对英语的了解，"洋文"的大门敞开了，西方诗歌的殿堂能稍作窥探，而不至于神秘莫测、误读误解（他们并非学者、译者，但相较某些继续不求甚解、以讹传讹的大陆诗歌翻译出版物，可谓清流）。于是更有另一个反转：华裔诗人的汉语也有了让英语世界阅读的必要和条件。这是因为，华裔诗人是所居住地区的一员，他们的观察、反思，他们的诗情、语言，融入英语阅读的世界之后，就与当地的文化、诗人分享了。人类的共情性，通过诗人的互通性来实现，比以政治和战争的手段，以商业与贸易的方式，应该更具有价值。这就是我们选编部分美国华裔诗人的诗歌作品并翻译为英文，在美国纽约出版的缘由。类似的选集和翻译与出版，这几年做了多次，这本双语作品集，自然也不会是殿军之作。

实际上，这本双语诗集是我们日常生活和多元文化的一种自然延续：在美国生活和工作多年，这样一种经验绝对是很寻常的，即和美国同事的交谈中，性之所至，把自己的诗翻译并朗读给他们听，并得到非常正面的反应，这要比聊天气、论时事，更具力度和丰富性，也更容易加深彼此的理解。

这本书的汉语原作，还具有一个唯有在美国才会显得正常的现象：繁体和简体并存。因为诗人的背景和爱好，他们写作时惯用不同的字"体"。我们尊重并保留了他们的用法。无论在中国大陆还是台湾，你阅读的汉语书，绝对不会有此种现象。这与其是一种"不规范"，毋宁是汉语书写在海外的独特表达，也增加了读者阅读的多样性感受。

邱辛晔

2024.7

PREFACE

As soon as it took birth, modern Chinese poetry faced awkward circumstances that were only a foretaste of the vicissitudes it would pass through during its first century of development. Modern poetry was part of the May 4th Cultural and Literature Movement that began in 1919. Right from when the first line of new poetry was written, its mission was to shake up tradition and loosen the grip of classical language. Most of its pioneers and advocates were stoked with radical fervor that imagined poetic lines as swords or plowshares, and they didn't shrink back from rough, brash gestures. At the same time, writers of the new poetry inhaled large lungfuls of air from Western literature. Some of them read original works, but most of them read in translation. The muscularity of the latter medium made it a powerful influence in its own right, to the point that modern poetry in China, in its early stage, guzzled infusions of translated literature like a medicinal tonic. The result was the creation of poems in a truly vernacular medium; from their marrow to their external lineaments they embodied dual characteristics of cosmopolitanism and accessibility. Readers and poets who know the history of modern poetry in China are quite familiar with this. Of course, we are not saying that modern poetry in China was entirely characterized by plainness and straight- forwardness. On its developmental path of experimentation and innovation, it passed through its own "Lake-Side" and "Symbolist" phases.[*1] During the 1930s and 1940s, the "Modern," "Seventh Month" and "Nine Leaves" groups formed a triumvirate. All of them adopted paradigms that were clearly traceable to Western literary models. From the 1950s onward, while poetry of Mainland China followed its own path of social realism, modern Taiwan poetry spawned an exuberant variety of schools and great numbers of individual practitioners. In the hands of Taiwan poets, the Chinese language grew increasingly mature as a vehicle for poetic sensibility. The awkward vestiges of "translationese" were cleansed from the vernacular language, and poetry was once again able to absorb reserves from its own classical heritage. Meanwhile on the Mainland, modern poetry did not re-appear with new force until over twenty years later (after the Cultural Revolution). In its new symbolist form as "Misty Poetry," and in a proliferation of new groups beginning with "Today" and "First Line," Mainland poetry demonstrated its phoenix-like emergence from its previous hobbling constraints, until a steady stream of originality from the early 1980s onward, enabled it to hold its own with poetry from the other side of the Taiwan Strait.

The poetry journal *Yi-hang* ["First Line"], founded in New York City in 1987, was an emigre vehicle that opened the way for creative practice that was true to the substance of Chinese-language poetry, along with a renaissance of poetic spirit. Because of its unique position overseas, in a setting that enjoyed freedom of publication, Mainland Chinese poets and overseas Chinese poets were able to display their strengths alongside each other. The eclectic magazine format provided space for over a thousand poets to establish themselves. This had a tremendous influence on members of poetry groups back on the Mainland before they eventually set up their own unofficial journals. At the core of *First Line 's* lineage lay a concern for universal human values and reflection on all the multifarious doings of human beings. The original *First Line* shouldered the responsibility to preserve a record of contemporary affairs in poetic voices. Such a commitment deserves to be extended and carried on. In 2019, after being inactive for more than ten years, *First Line* resumed publication under the new name *Niuyue-Yihang* ["New York First Line"]. As a quarterly of poetry and art, available in a printed format, it has by now published 14 issues. It is distributed to literary circles in China and abroad, and it is collected by libraries. At the same time, it has put out nearly 100 issues of a biweekly electronic periodical, providing a space for hundreds of poets to be seen by readers. From 1987 to 2000, the original *First Line* was a reliable non-official publication which poets in Mainland China could rely on and look up to, because its overseas location freed it from restrictions that limited other journals. As a point of difference between that original journal and the new *New York First Line*, although Mainland poets still regard the latter with enthusiasm, many who submit their work are overseas Chinese living in America, Europe, and other places around the world. As they continue to write poetry in Chinese, the mother tongue becomes their both their spiritual homeland and the basis of their independent outlook, even though many of them also have a strong command of English. At this point, the vernacular Chinese poetry movement, after over 100 years, seems to have arrived at a new inflection point. For emigre Chinese poets, in the course of their long sojourns abroad, the door to the English language has opened. They have access to Western literature at the source, and they no longer need to treat it as a mysterious subject to haphazard misreadings. (They are not scholars or translators, but they have a clearer view than those poorly informed Mainland translators who continue to perpetuate botched and misconstrued readings.) This brings us to another inflection point. The Chinese written by emigre poets by now has content that deserves and needs to be read by English-language readers. This is because emigre Chinese poets are socially involved in their place of habitation; each has observations and reflections and poetic language that has something to offer to the culture and poets of that area, once it is incorporated into a corpus of readable material in English. Human beings have a common ground of affectivity which is manifested when poets connect with each other. This connection has greater intrinsic value than that achieved through political means or armed conflict, or even by the exchange of commodities. This is why we have made a selection of material by emigre Chinese poets and arranged to have it translated into English and published in New York. We have prepared a number of such selections in recent years, and we will definitely not treat the preparation of the current volume as a rearguard action.

In fact, this bilingual poetry volume is a natural extension of our everyday cultural pluralism. For those of us who have lived and worked for years in America, such an experience is absolutely ordinary. In conversations with co-workers, when the spirit moves us, to recite one's own translated poems to them, and then hear their frank, positive responses, is richer and more powerful than exchanging remarks about the weather or current events. It is also more likely to deepen our mutual understanding.

In this book's original Chinese texts, there is another phenomenon that could only appear in America: poems in simplified and regular Chinese characters are mingled together. Depending on the individual poet's background and preference, we use the "type" of characters that he/she habitually writes in. We honor and preserve the usage of whichever writing system he/she chooses. Whether you read Chinese books from Mainland China or from Taiwan, you will never not find a book that mingles the two systems together this way. Rather than say this phenomenon is "irregular," we prefer to say it is a unique expression of Chinese-language writing overseas. What is more, for those who read it, it gives a greater sense of multiplicity.

Qiu Xinye
Co-Founder and Executive Director of Flushing Poetry Festival, New York
July 2024

[*1] *Note: The English "Lake Poets" were a group that was active in England's Lake District in the first half of the 19th century. This group included William Wordsworth, Robert Southey, Samuel Taylor Coleridge and Charles Lamb. In 1922 a group of Chinese poets whose penchant for passionate outpourings was reminiscent of the English romantics formed a "Lake-Side Poetry Society" by the shores of West Lake in Hangzhou.]*

译者简介

Denis Mair（梅丹理），美国诗人，中英文翻译者，俄亥俄州立大学中文硕士。曾担任台湾涵静学院研究员，美国宾州大学东亚语文系讲师。译作包括真华法师《参学琐谭》（纽约州立大学出版社，1992）、冯友兰《三松堂全集自序》（夏威夷大学出版社，2000）、朱朱《一幅画的诞生》（湖南美术出版社）。诗歌翻译包括《麦城诗选》（伦敦 Shearsman Books，2009）；马悦然编《台湾新诗选》（哥仑比亚大学出版社，2005）；吉狄马加《黑色狂欢曲》（俄克拉荷马大学出版社，2014）；骆英《文革记忆》（俄克拉荷马大学出版社，2015）；杨克《地球苹果的两半》（俄克拉荷马大学出版社，2017）；还有当代诗人严力、孟浪等。其个人英文诗集《木刻里的人》于 2004 年由洛杉矶 Valley Contemporary Poets 出版。

Denis Mair: Brief bio

Denis Mair holds an M.A. in Chinese from Ohio State University and has taught as lecturer at Whitman College and University of Pennsylvania. He was research fellow for many years at Hanching Academy (Sun Moon Lake), and served as translator for Jidi Majia (Deputy Chair, Chinese Writers Association). Denis translated books by the Buddhist monk Shih Chen-hua (SUNY Albany, 1992), the philosopher Feng Youlan (Hawaii University, 2000), and the art critic Zhu Zhu (Hunan Fine Arts, 2009). His poetry translations include: *Frontier Taiwan* (Columbia University Press, 2005); *Contemporary Chinese Poetry* (Shanghai Literary Arts, 2007); Yan Zhi, *Reading the Times* (Homa & Sekey, 2012); Jidi Majia, *Rhapsody in Black* (Univ. of Oklahoma, 2014); Luo Ying, *Memories of the Cultural Revolution* (Univ. of Oklahoma, 2015); Yang Ke, *Two Halves of the World Apple* (Univ. of Oklahoma, 2017), as well as *7+2 Mountain Climber's Journal* (White Pine, 2020). He has also translated poetry by Yan Li, Meng Lang and many others. His own poetry collection *Man Cut in Wood* was published by Valley Contemporary Poets (Los Angeles, 2004).

目　　录
Table of Contents

寒山老藤/ Hanshan Laoteng

居住在纽约布鲁克林的华语诗人,
作品散发在一些电子刊物和纸媒。
在诗的写作上,尝试用中国诗传
统中的简洁和含蓄手法,来表达
西方文学中的人性思考。

Hanshan Laoteng (Cold-Mountain Old
-Vine) is a Chinese-speaking poet living
in Brooklyn, New York. His works are
distributed in electronic publications
and paper media. "In the writing of
poetry, I try to use the concise and
implicit techniques from the Chinese
poetry tradition to express the thinking
about human nature in Western
literature."

雪

有关雪景的构想
早在秋末 就被定稿了
何时下雪
由不得我

也由不得雪
下雪的意义 不单是为了
凸显 那一溜领路的足印
但有时候 不得不是

特别是 逼退了
红极一时的枫叶后
营造一场 全票通过的冬雪
成了一件 良心事

雪也无法拒绝 春暖花开后
地上 只留下一滩污名
命运属于自己
成败 却由不得自己

2023 年 11 月 26 日

Snow

Already in late fall, my visions of snowy scenes
were in their final draft
When the snow would fall
was not up to me

and it wasn't not up to the snow either
Snow's meaning is not just to highlight
a line of footprints that guide the way ahead
but sometimes that's what they must do

especially after forcing maple leaves to withdraw,
with their color that was all the rage for a time
setting winter's stage for a unanimous yes to snow
achieving something in a cause of conscience

Once spring warmth brings flowers, the snow
must give way, leaving its sullied name on the land
Fate is apportioned to everyone
victory or defeat is not up to oneself

Nov. 26, 2023

简 约

经康定斯基风一吹
线条和色块　便在想象中活了
那些不堪的经历和暗黑
也被想象　引到了哲学的入口

好事的简约主义者　删减了
雨水落入城市的情节
从天空掉入屋顶　流入水沟
入海前　先同流合污

就像我　入世前
始料未及的那样
如此简约　不容遮掩
像裸露的人生　一点也不抽象主义

2023 年 10 月 21 日

Minimal

Having been through a gust of Kandinsky's wind
lines and colors come alive in imagination
Unbearable happenings and dark times are brought
by imagination's guidance to philosophy's door

A minimalist, looking for things to do, has deleted
the plot points of rain that poured down on the city
It falls from the sky over roofs and into ditches
dirtied by where it flows before entering the sea

Just as I, before I entered into worldly matters
which changed me in ways I couldn't expect
was my pared-down self, with nothing to hide
a naked human life, not a subject for abstraction

Oct. 21, 2023

窗 后

他们的灵魂
隔着皮囊
他们的咖啡 和喜怒哀乐
隔着玻璃
我站在窗后 看着街道
仿佛秋风 只凋零路人

在窗后 像一只
被遗忘的陶罐
没人知道我的存在 之后
也没人知道 我已不存在
仿佛 路人在剧本里
在此刻 只有灵魂正悄悄靠近

2023 年 11 月 3 日

At a Window

Their souls are kept apart
by separate bags of flesh
Their coffee and their succession of moods
are separated by glass
I stand at a window, watching a street scene
as if only passers-by wilt and fade in the fall wind

Standing at a widow, looking like
a clay jar that was forgotten
no one knows of my existence, and later
no one will know of my non-existence
as if passers-by were written into a play and
at this moment, only the soul draws near them

Nov. 3, 2023

一初/ Yi Chu

祖籍湖南岳阳，旅居南达科他州的一个小乡村，出版有英文诗集《凡心》，早年于广州日报，微型文学，洞庭文联发表过诗和散文。擅长油画，生活美学，诗词，散文，小说。喜欢抒写自然与乡村，以及生活经历感受和爱情诗，遵从大道至简。

Yi Chu's ancestral home was Yueyang, Hunan, and she lives in a small village in South Dakota. She published an English poetry collection *Ordinary Heart*. In her early years, she published poems and prose in *Guangzhou Daily*, *Micro Literature*, and *Dongting Literary Magazine*. Good at oil painting, life aesthetics, poetry, prose, and novels. "I like to write about nature and countryside, as well as life experiences and love poems, and follow the principle of simplicity."

爱的卑微

我是结着雨的云朵
当你伫立在芭蕉前
我便落在你的肩上
湿漉漉的望着你

我是盈盈的一道晓风
在你转过身的刹那
轻轻的擦过你的眼眸

我是那池子里的秋水
当你低头朝向我
就如同万剑穿胸
激起不能停息的
漩涡和哀痛

Lowly Love

I'm a cloud bearing the rain as fruit
When you stand by a row of plantain trees
I fall upon your shoulders
and look at you wetly

I am a buoyant gust of morning wind
at the moment that you turn about
I lightly brush the corner of your eye

I am the pond's water, swollen in autumn
When you lower your head towards me
many swords seem to pierce my chest
These waters are stirred to restlessness
and grief that comes in eddies

假 若

假若爱是一个假命题
我将毫不犹豫的和你一起蹈火
哪怕炼成金身

我带着铁锹和雪花的种子来了
还有前世今生的枯萎和流浪

留一扇春天的门楣
让我的月光在那里浮动

没有翅膀的鱼
将自己安顿在水里

我将埋在你山脉上
被你连绵不断的爱意养着

打江南
一次次经过

一直婉约
一直忍住小悲伤

Suppose That…

Suppose that love were a contrafactual assumption
I would join you to tread upon fire without hesitation
even if it meant tempering my body to metal

I have come bringing a shovel and snowflakes as seeds
with my withering and rootlessness from many lifetimes

Leave the lintel of springtime's door
for my moonlight to wax and wane upon

A fish without wings
finds a place for itself in the water

I will be buried in your mountain range
to be nourished by your love that stretches far

One who comes from the Yangtze
will pass by again and again

Always showing graceful restraint
always enduring minor sorrows

左拉/ Zora

本名万颖龄，公共管理硕士，美国科技和医疗机构高管。自幼习画，爱好文字。作品在纽约一行、奴隶社会和休士顿诗苑等期刊均有发表。著有诗画集《不惑之旅》和插画书《Eye of the Dragon》。更多关于作者和作品信息请见 zorawanart.com

Zora, whose real name is Wan Yingling, holds a master's degree in public administration and is an executive of American technology and medical institutions. She has studied painting since childhood and loves writing. Her works have been published in periodicals such as *First Line New York*, *Slave Society*, and *Houston Poetry Garden*. She is the author of the poetry and painting collection *The Journey of No Confusion* and the illustrated book *Eye of the Dragon*. More information about the author and work can be found at zorawanart.com

时光的河流

时光在我们的身体上流过
留下山丘峡谷
时光在我们的面颊上流过
把平湖变成沙漠
时光在我们的心间流过
将爱掩埋于沉默

时光的河流慢慢地流淌
过去从未过去
只是留在了上游
无法追溯遥不可及
却在手指相触瞬间
却在四目相视之间
打开了一扇窗

时光的河流慢慢地流淌
将来已经发生
只是发生在下游
黑暗光明或不可知
却在掌心画上了手纹
却在心间埋下了愿望
像北极星在指引方向

时光的河流慢慢地流淌
现在正骑着白马

深陷河流的当场
无处可躲无处可藏
唯有与它一同呼吸
让感官完全开张
让宇宙扑面而入
让心随波逐浪

一切归于静寂
时光的河流慢慢地流淌

The River of Passing Time

The river of time flows over our bodies
leaving rolling hills or maybe canyons
The river of time flows over our faces
a placid lake may turn into a desert
The river of time flows over our hearts
burying love in silence

The river of time slows to a trickle
the past is never really past
it only remains upstream
too hard to trace, too far to touch
but it is there in the moment two hands touch
it opens a window
when eyes meet eyes

The river of time slows to a trickle
The future has already happened
even though the happening is downstream
Darkness and light may be hard to know
but their marks are drawn in a palmprint
Their wishes are buried in hearts
like the pole star guiding our course

The river of time slows to a trickle
a moment of full immersion in the flow

comes riding a white horse onto the scene
There is nowhere to hide oneself away
The only way is to breathe together with it
to throw open the organs of perception
to plunge into the cosmos head on
to flow where the waves take you

Everything ends up in stillness
The river of time slows to a trickle

春天哭泣

春天扶着屋顶哭泣
噼里啪啦
叫起了深梦初醒的人
它哭喊着
冲淡了在冬天酝酿太久的阴郁
熄灭了加州森林里累积的燥动

春天摸着窗户哭泣
淅淅沥沥的眼泪
把向往太阳的心
囚在了屋里
像在导演一场祭祀
祭奠着
一朵只留在记忆里的微笑
一个陷入黑暗的身影
一段无法追溯的阳光灿烂的日子

春天搂着金发红唇的妻子哭泣
谁不爱白头到老儿女成行
为什么你要放他去自投罗网
世界总是对称的
心灵总是可以选择
有多少自私
就有多少正直
黑暗和光明同在于心

春天掩面而泣
是为满是勇气赴往火焰的人儿流泪
还是为被欲望拽进黑洞的人儿悲哀

春天大声的哭
洗遍大地上滚烫的心灵

3/2024

Springtime Is Crying

Springtime leans against the roof and cries
that blustery stir rouses the one
who was just climbing out of a dream
Its wailing cries dispel a long winter's gloom
quelling the pent-up restlessness of a California forest

Spring's sobs rub against the winter
its constant drizzling tears
keep a sunlight-loving heart
imprisoned inside a house, as if
to carry out a ceremonial offering
That which is offered will be
a smile that only remained in memory
a silhouette that receded into darkness
a span of sunny days that can't be recovered

Sobbing spring hugs a gold-haired, red-lipped wife
Who wouldn't want to grow old together, children all around?
Why did you let that one go, to be snared in fate's trap alone?
The world always lines up in symmetries
A sensitive heart can always make a choice
For any amount of selfishness, there is also
the same amount of uprightness
Darkness and light share the same heart

Springtime covers its face and weeps
shedding tears for one who bravely strode into fire
grieving for one who was pulled into desire's black hole

Springtime cries out loud, to cleanse them all
those hotly churning hearts all over the world

March 2024

陆地鱼/ Land Fish

本名肖颖。生于北京，
长于安徽。理工博士。
现居美国西雅图，从事
能源工作。热爱文字，
诗歌曾获 2018 北美首届
法拉盛诗歌节一等奖。

Land Fish, whose real name is
Xiao Ying, was born in
Beijing and raised in Anhui;
holds a Doctorate in
Engineering. Now living in
Seattle, USA, working in the
energy industry. She loves
words, and her poetry won
first prize at the first New
York Flushing Poetry Festival
in 2018.

国庆日与儿子在海边

天边，七月的蓝色鼓点浩荡
召唤滑板少年的翅膀
你的衣衫鼓起，像新生的海螺
渴望被风呜呜吹响

——我知道，你终将成为
异乡人，如同多年前的我
这无疑是一种宿命
恍若轮回

世界那么大，我想象不出
有多少星球在你脚下展开
你将举出多少迷失于风暴的岛屿
又将推开多少扇窗，眺望

时光漫散，鱼群在深海投下倒影
你的航线坚定，有如
一场回归，任所有遗留在岸上的
独自老去

每一次停靠，只要你回望
挥手，就会有风
打着旋向我扑面而来
——如同此刻一样

每一个迎风流泪的人啊
我爱你们

7/4/2018

At the Beach with My Son on July 4th

At the sky's edge, July's blue drumbeats advance grandly
summoning youthful surfers on wings of foam
Your shirt bellies out like a pristine conch shell
eager for the wind to sound its trumpet

I know someday you'll become an outlander
just as I did many years ago
this is doubtlessly ordained by destiny
as if on the wheel of reincarnation

The world is so huge, I cannot imagine
how many stars will pave the way for your feet
how many islets you will raise out of storms
how many windows you'll open to gaze afar

At each moorage, if only you look back and wave
a wind will whirl back to brush my face
—just as one is whirling now

to those who face the wind with teary eyes
I love all of you

July 4, 2018

雪是一场救赎

每个早晨，阳光从背后穿过我
—— 傍晚也是。在此之间
它是完全敞开的，俯视
垂落金黄的叶片

那些叶片也落在你睡梦的额上
风就要牵着它们跑过来了——
然而，你比诞生宇宙的潮水还要遥远
我甚至无法用一只柑橘的气息来触及

如同这个秋天，那只南半球的蝴蝶
是真实的，它不安的心跳也是
更真实的是，火山在海底膨胀
时间窒息于欢愉

那些预言即将水落石出
而我们浑然不觉

我赤裸双足，行走于火焰之中
你一说起雪，雪就下起来了
雪是钟声坠落一瞬生出的翅膀
—— 雪是救赎，雪是多年后的遗忘

11/12/2017

Snowfall Is a Time of Redemption*

At daybreak sunlight shines through me from behind
and in the evening likewise. Between the two times
the sky is totally open to the light, looking down on
the withering and falling of gold leaves

Some of them fall towards your sleeping forehead
the wind tugging them is about to rush this way, but you
are farther away than water from which the cosmos was born
I cannot even touch it with the scent of a tangerine

Like the butterfly this fall, from the southern hemisphere
it was actual, as was its uneasy heartbeat
Even more actual is a swelling volcano on the seafloor
and the suffocation of time by amusements

What was prophesied will emerge like rocks in a riverbed
as we go about our business, not really noticing

I go barefoot, proceeding on foot amid flames
No sooner do you speak of snow, than it starts falling
Snowflakes are wings, born in the moment a bell starts tolling
Snow is redemption; snow is forgetting after many years

*[In Chinese, the image of snow can be used as a metaphor for
redress or vindication. (Tr)]

Nov. 12, 2017

春天里

满世界都在开花
（也许只有花
才能让这春光不再可疑）
我发现，我正在长刺
悲悯与愤怒有同样的锋芒

—— 我期待长出更多的刺
我也期待，每个人都长出刺
因为这跪伏的人间需要刺
就如同需要硬骨，盐和光

我开过太多温驯的花
在归于终级的死寂之前

我需要把一生中
该长的刺都长出来

淡忘索多玛的罪孽是可耻的
一个只允许开花的人世更为可耻

而那些长刺的
被刺扎得鲜血淋漓的人
他们终将死去
也终将生出救赎的翅膀

03/04/2020

In Springtime

The whole world is blooming
(perhaps only by virtue of flowers
is the coming of spring beyond a doubt)
I've found that I am growing thorns
compassion and fury alike have sharp edges

—— I look forward to growing even more thorns
I also look forward to everyone growing thorns, because
in this human world full of lurking things, thorns are needed
just as a strong spine and salt and light are needed

I've put forth too many delicate blooms
Before I end up reaching my ultimate cessation
I need to let all the thorns grow on me
that should have been growing on me

To let memories of Sodom's sins fade would be shameful
A world that only lets flowers bloom is more shameful

As for those who grow thorns
and are bloodied by sharp thorns
they will ultimately die, yet ultimately
they will grow wings of redemption

March 4, 2020

杨皓/ Yang Hao

美籍华裔诗人、艺术评论家、策展人、艺术品收藏家，纽约穆瑞山艺术博物馆(Murray Hill Art Museum)创办人、馆长，美国中国当代艺术基金会主席、Top 100 Collectors Group 主席。著有诗集《过河拆桥》（作家出版社）、艺术评论集《冒险的历程》（北京大学出版社）等。

Yang Hao, Chinese-American poet, art critic, curator, art collector, founder and director of the Murray Hill Art Museum in New York, chairman of the American Chinese Contemporary Art Foundation, Top 100 Collectors Group Chairman. He is the author of the poetry collection *Crossing the River and Burning the Bridge* (Writers Press), and the art criticism collection *The Journey of Adventures* (Peking University Press).

我在天上看著你

我在天上看着你
看着你长发及腰
看着你在海滩上奔跑
海风吹走了你的叹息
看着时间
把你追逐
看着你的白裙
飘啊飘

我在天上看着你
看着你的孤独
看着你在大海和陆地间旅行
一颗空心
一面面被修饰的笑颜
看着你的自尊
被风鼓起
让我读懂了
你的寂寞

我在天上看着你
我爱的美人儿
你倚在花园的香草中
岁月装饰着你的梦
也收起了你的笑容

我看着你的泪儿
也化着了香灰

我在天上看着你
看着镜子里刮起了狂风
那空心里
也掀起了波澜
看着你在苦苦寻觅
看着你的
孤独无依

I Am up in Heaven Watching You

I am up in heaven watching you
your long hair and your waist
I watch you run on a beach
as the wind blows your sighs away
I am watching you
as time pursues you
I watch your white skirt
tossed in the wind

I am up in heaven watching you
watching your loneliness
your travels between ocean and dry land
the emptiness of your heart
and the smiles you wear on your face
I watch your dignity
being summoned forth by the wind
by which I can read
the extent of your loneliness

I am up in heaven watching you
my beloved beauty
leaning beside a bed of fragrant herbs
Passing years enhance your dreams
but they do away with your smile
I see that even your tears

are being transformed
to incense ash

I am up in heaven watching you
watching the wild winds blowing
against your image in a mirror
and the waves they stir
in your empty heart
watching your long-suffering search
watching you in solitude
with nothing to rely on

纽约的一朵孤云

纽约的一朵孤云
有一颗孤星
隐藏在它的后面
她孤独冷艳
神秘地微笑着
俯看着纽约

她俯看着纽约
透过亿万光年的玻璃
她深情地俯看着
这人类奇特的实验室
她完全遗忘了
她所在的星系

从一滴水的倒影中
从一个婴儿的眼睛深处
我看见了那朵孤云
那颗孤星

A Lone Cloud over New York

A lone cloud over New York
has a lone star
hiding behind it
Solitary and coldly aloof
with a mysterious smile
peering down on the city

She surveys New York through the glass
of a hundred thousand light years
Gazing down with deep feeling
at humankind's uncanny laboratory
the thought of her own star system
totally slips her mind

From a reflection in a drop of water
and from deep in an infant's eye
I catch sight of that lone star
behind that lone cloud

给凡高的一封信

凡·高
自从我在阿尔
与你别后
我就处在一种
更深的抑郁里
如你所询
我亦住进一所
精神病院里
只是这里的设施
远比你住的那间豪华
我去过你的麦田
群鸦
没有再飞回来
向日葵的腰
更加佝偻了
在你流连过的圣雷米尔山上
橄榄在今年
普遍歉收
有些树枝，出于
对这个世界的积怨
不愿结出果实
我看见吊桥下
有一些死鱼
在我们喝咖啡的酒馆外面
有个年轻人
表情非常彷徨

凡·高
你几号跟我去中国？
那里有你的
很多传记
正睁着失神的眼睛
有些已经发了霉
雨天可能会
加重你的病情
你别再生高更的气
好吗
他要去大溪地
你就让他去吧
他可能还要
去马丁尼克岛
我们一起去武汉
去北京和上海

凡·高
自从我在阿尔
与你别后
你就不曾离开过我
我的病情
还在加深之中
希望你多些耐心
让我躲过
这个雨季……

A Letter to Van Gogh

Van Gogh
Ever since I said farewell
to you in Arles
a deeper melancholy
has come over me
In reply to your question
I too have been admitted
to a mental health ward
except that the facilities here
are fancier than yours
I went to your wheat fields
but the flock of crows did not return
The waists of sunflowers
were even more hunched
The olive groves where you lingered
on the hills at Saint-Rémy,
are producing less than ever
Many of their branches
are unwilling to bear fruit
due to outrage at this world
Beneath the Langlois Drawbridge
I saw dead fish floating
Outside of the hotel where we had coffee
there was a young man
in the throes of anomie

Van Gogh
when will you go with me to China
There are many copies of your biography there
you gaze distractedly from the covers
some are growing mold in the dampness
The rainy season there
may aggravate your condition
Wouldn't it be better
not to be so angry at Gaugin?
If he wants to go to Tahiti
let him go, even if
he continues on from there
to Martinique as well
We can go to Wuhan together
then to Beijing and Shanghai

Van Gogh
After you and I
said goodbye at Arles
you have never left me
My condition
is also getting serious
I hope you'll be patient
and let me get through
this rainy season

双一/ Shuangyi

本名杨靖海，旅居夏威夷，著有诗集《走在地上的人》。作品见于《纽约一行》《创世纪》《新大陆》《中国诗歌》《国际诗坛》等多种诗刊，被收入多种诗歌选本与年鉴。曾获纽约法拉盛诗歌节一等奖，汉新文学奖，全球华语诗歌奖等。

Shuangyi, whose real name is Yang Jinghai, lives in Hawaii and is the author of the poetry collection *People Walking on the Earth*. His works have appeared in various poetry magazines such as *First Line New York, Genesis, New World, Chinese Poetry, International Poetry,* and have been included in various poetry anthologies and yearbooks. He has won the first prize at the New York Flushing Poetry Festival, as well as the Sino Literature Award and the Global Chinese Poetry Award.

回答

这段日子，衣带宽了。
走路慢了。脚步深了。
生命的忧患，在这段日子，凝成巨石。
我是挑石之人

我们都是挑石之人。
墓园里的石碑是证明：
那些石头从肩膀卸下来，终于
立在躺平的身前

湖面漂着我佝偻的倒影
游弋的鱼穿过
我想和鱼交换身体
失重一样在水里浮游

我在岸上看鱼
天上有没有一双眼睛看我？

"我的轭是容易的，我的担子是轻省的"
这是天空给我的回答。
他一直想和我交换身体，只是我不懂
像鱼不懂，我为何弯曲着脊梁

Answer

This span of days, my belt has gotten looser.
Walking gets slower, steps trudge more heavily.
Cares and sorrows, these days, solidify to stones.
I'm a carrier of stones

we are all carriers of stones.
Headstones in the graveyard are proof:
those stones on the shoulder at last unloaded
placed in front of a body lying flat

My hunched reflection is suspended
on the lake's surface; fish swishing their tails
pass through it; I want to exchange bodies with a fish
and glide through water as if in free fall

I'm on the bank watching fish
Does the sky have a pair of eyes to watch me?

"My yoke is easy, and my burden is light."
This is the answer the sky gives. It has been wanting
to trade bodies with me, but I don't understand
just as fish don't understand why I hunch my spine

重奏

日子被大海推涌成起伏的曲线
我们是曲线上的音符
时间悠长的琴弦，一个爆破音
与休止符，之间
切分、停顿、渐强、渐弱的一段
就是我们
我们垒起城堡在沙滩
用脚印标记方向
我们的呼喊融入海水轰鸣的乐章
抱着木质理想的勇敢者
从岸边冲向大海
收获的海浪把他从大海推回岸边
往返来去，意义的手指画出节拍
我们斜倚的红日落入海之摇篮的
夜晚，海用呼吸擦拭琴弦
一些音符对视黑暗醒着
一些音符歪着头颅睡去

Refrain

The days are stirred by the vast sea into troughs and crests
We are notes upon those undulating curves
On time's lingering violin string, between bursts of sound
and rests, all the pauses and syncopation
the diminuendos and crescendos
are what comprise us
We put up castle walls on a sand beach
We mark our direction with footprints
Our cries merge into the sea's seething allegro
and the bold ones who stake lives on steadfastness of wood
strike out from shore, charging into the open sea
until harvest-giving waves push them back onto shore
to and fro they go; the finger of purpose traces out a rhythm
We lean towards the red sun that sets in the sea's blue cradle
at night, and the ocean strokes violin strings with it breath
Some wakeful notes stare darkness in the face
Some notes slump their heads and fall asleep

沉默之诗

这一次，古拉格群岛抓捕的是词语
它们犯下白纸罪和屏幕罪

从嘴边逃脱的词语消失于风
在手指被捉住的是自投罗网

果实落入篮子，星光收进眼睛
词语诚实的归宿是高墙

公共舞台上扭动的，都腰膝酸软
掀开透明衣服的，转入精神病房

如果从星光与果实我了解天地的良善
那么从词语我学习写沉默的诗

是的，沉默。词语的乱葬岗没有墓碑
即便有，也将空无一字

我将我的诗埋入地下
我要让我的词语做沉默的雷

A Poem of Silence

This time, the Gulag Archipelago imprisons words
for crimes committed against blank paper and screens

Words that escape the lips disappear in the wind
Those caught by the fingers submit themselves to the net

Fruits fallen into a basket, starlight gathered into eyes
The resting place of honesty in words is a high wall

Those gyrating on a public stage get sore in the waist and knees
Those flouncing about in negligees are bound for a mental ward

If I come to know nature's goodness by fruit and starlight
then from words I learn to write poems of silence

Yes, silence. On the charnel hill of words there are few
gravestones
and even if there are, the inscriptions are mostly effaced

I bury my poems in the ground there
I want my words to make silent thunder

黑丰/ Hei Feng

诗人，作家。著
作：诗集《空孕》
《灰烬之上》《猫
的两个夜晚》《时
间深轧》等，实验
小说集《蝴蝶是这
个下午的一半》、
随笔集《一切的底
部》《存在一闪
烁》等。获奖：罗
马尼亚阿尔杰什国

际诗歌节特别荣誉奖、雅西第6届国际诗歌节历史首都诗人奖；ASA
大学纽约国际文化艺术节贡献奖、纽约法拉盛诗歌节汉诗翻译奖等。
中国第四届青年华语作家奖、北京白雀奖等重要奖项的评委和终审
评委。

Hei Feng, poet, writer. Works: poetry collections *Empty Pregnancy, Above the Ashes, Two Nights of the Cat, The Deep Passage of Time,* etc.; experimental novel collection *Butterflies Are Half of the Afternoon;* essay collections *The Bottom of Everything* and *Existence-Flicker.* Awards: Special Honor Award at the Arges International Poetry Festival in Romania, Historic Capital Poet Award at the 6th International Poetry Festival in Iasi; ASA University New York International Culture and Arts Festival Contribution Award, New York Flushing Poetry Festival Chinese Poetry Translation Award. He is a judge and final judge for important awards such as the 4th China Young Chinese Writers Award and the Beijing White Bird Award.

别

加一滴苦泪
加一点盐　甚至可以
加进一点地沟油

别让佛灯
太空
太飘渺
别让佛陀太凄清

2018.8.19

Don't

You can add a bitter teardrop
add a bit of salt; you can even
add oil drained from a kitchen gutter

Just don't let the votive lamp
get too empty
don't let the flame
start guttering too much
don't let the Buddha feel too forlorn

Aug. 2018

一颗孤独的钉子

这里的每一颗钉子
都是她一人敲进去的

每一颗钉子都无助
每一颗钉子都孤勇

每一颗钉子都是一个人的钉子
每一颗钉子都是一个滴血的人

喋血建屋，建一个女人的居所
建一个人的心房，做梦、不漂泊

2023.1.22 紐約

A Solitary Nail

Every single nail here
was pounded in by her, all alone

Each nail was driven in helplessness
Each nail was driven in valor

Each nail is the nail of one person only
Each nail is the nail of one who sheds blood

To build takes loss of blood, to build a woman's dwelling
to build a heart's nest for dreams, do be done with drifting

Jan. 22, 2023 in New York

苏拉/ Su-la

诗人，现居新泽西。诗作
发表于新大陆，一行，诗
刊，幸存者等。获2022诗
歌岛年度推荐诗人。著诗
集《他世之花》。

Su-la, poet, now lives in New
Jersey. Poems have been
published in *New World, First
Line New York, Poetry Magazine,
Survivor*, etc. Recommended
poet of the year by the Poetry
Island website in 2022. Author
of poetry collection *Flowers of
Other Worlds*.

我想生活在火焰中

我想生活在火焰中
火焰的指环，火焰的房子，
火之书中
非线性的字体。
将一面是身体
一面是灵魂的硬币熔化，
非生非死。
每种药创造一种新的疾病，
更高的火苗
扑向每一次注视。
赤裸的瑜伽士在雪顶忍耐极寒
抵抗着欲念与矛盾，
而我将在火焰中沉迷
跟随她感性的舞姿。
秘密是超越，而不是选择。

I Want to Live within Flames

I want to live within flames, with a ring
of flame on my finger, in a room of flame;
within books of flame there is
a print font with no straight lines.
Half will be body, and half
the melted currency of soul,
neither on the side of life nor death.
Each kind of medicine creates a new sickness,
and higher tongues of flame pounce forth
each time I am gazed at. A stark naked yogi
bears the harsh chill on a snowy peak
resisting the contradictions of desire.
But I will immerse myself in flame
following her emotive dance steps. A secret
that wins transcendence leaves you no choice

日 蚀

墨西哥人曾教我
透过黑曜石片观察太阳。
数亿爆发的耀斑，
高速抛射的日冕物质，
投射成黑石中一轮柔软，
昏黄的幻影。

我也是一个梦吗？
被一个耀眼的神梦了一千年。
如复原的日蚀苏醒，
呢喃着
我又完整了。

Solar Eclipse

Mexicans once taught me
to observe the sun through obsidian lenses.
Hundreds of millions of solar plasma cells erupt
in high-velocity ejections of coronal mass,
shining through black glass as a soft annular ring,
a smudgy yellow illusion.

Am I also a dream? Has a dazzling god
dreamt me into existence over the past thousand years?
Awakening, like the eclipsed sun re-emerging
I am murmuring
as I become whole again.

云中雀/ Yunzhong-que

本名 Jason Xu，洛杉矶华文作家协会会员，首届纽约法拉盛诗歌节一等奖获得者。2020 年《美篇》最佳评委奖。2021 年获南加州诗歌类比赛一等奖。作品发表于《读者》《长江诗歌》《洛城诗刊》《纽约一行》，以及侨报和世界日报等。

Yunzhong-que (Lark-in-the-Clouds), whose real name is Jason Xu, is a member of the Los Angeles Chinese Writers Association and the first prize winner of the first New York Flushing Poetry Festival; 2020 *Mei Pian Best Judges' Award*. Won first prize in the Southern California Poetry Competition in 2021. His works were published in *Reader* and *Yangtze River Poetry*. *LA Poetry Magazine, First Line New York, China Press* and *World Journal*, etc.

我喜欢你斜躺的样子

窗外，你躺成几何线条
一条腿自然伸直
一条腿拱成三角形
健硕的双臂后摆 45 度
荷尔蒙倾斜……

光勾勒你挺拔的鼻峰
花海在脚下奔涌
一本诗集被风张满了帆
要有一只帝王蝶
屈服那双高傲的膝盖

但我喜欢你此刻
斜躺的样子
构成一架斜拉桥
桥上许一个紫衣女子
穿过你巨大的竖琴

I Like the Look of You Lying on Your Side

Outside the window, you are laid out
in geometrical lines
one leg stretched straight
one arched in a 90 degree angle
sturdy arms bent at 45 degree angles
setting my hormones raging

The sun highlights the high bridge of your nose
a sea of flowers tosses at your feet
wind spreads the sails of a poetry book
It would take a monarch butterfly
to make the pride of your knees submit

But this is what I like at this moment
the look of you lying on your side
assuming the outline of a suspension bridge
on which the figure of a woman dressed in purple
passes over the giant cello of your body

河岸印象

多年以后
马驮着我回来了
倒影变成水纹斑马
流水潺潺，我没说话
马也没有说话

水中，我驮着马
漂行在云河上
我们四脚朝天，看见
蓝天驮着白云
也没有说话。

Impressions on a Riverbank

After so many years
a horse carries me back
its zebra-like reflection striped by ripples
amid purling of water, I say nothing
the horse, too, says nothing

In the water, I am carrying the horse
adrift on a river of clouds
our feet are pointing skyward, where I see
the blue sky carrying white clouds
and they too say nothing.

王家新/ Wang Jiaxin

诗人、批评家、译者，1957 年
生于湖北省丹江口市，高中毕
业后下放劳动，"文革"结束
后考入武汉大学中文系，2006
年起被中国人民大学文学院聘
任为教授（现退休）。著有诗
集、诗论随笔集和译诗集四、
五十种，其中包括德文诗选
《晚来的献诗》、英文诗选
《变暗的镜子》、克罗地亚文
诗选《夜行火车》、荷兰文诗
选《黎明的灰烬》等，曾获多
种国内外诗歌奖、诗学批评奖
和翻译奖。近年来旅居纽约，
应邀在阿姆斯特丹做驻留作家，在美国和加拿大一些大学、文学节、
文学中心和图书馆讲学和朗诵。

Wang Jiaxin, poet, critic, and translator, was born in Danjiangkou City, Hubei
Province in 1957. After graduating from high school, he was transferred to the
labor force. After the "Cultural Revolution", he was admitted to the Chinese
Department of Wuhan University. In 2006, he was appointed as a professor by
the School of Liberal Arts of Renmin University of China (now retired). He has
authored 40 to 50 collections of poems, poetry essays and translated poems,
including the German poetry anthology *Poems of Late Arrival*, the English poetry
anthology *Darkening Mirror*, the Croatian poetry anthology *Night Train*, His Dutch
poetry anthology *Ashes of Dawn* and other works have won various domestic and
foreign poetry awards, poetic criticism awards and translation awards. In recent
years, he has lived in New York and was invited to be a writer-in-residence in
Amsterdam. He has lectured and recited at some universities, literary festivals,
literary centers and libraries in the United States and Canada.

波士顿的地铁——给哈金

满头白发，经过了中国东北
和新英格兰双倍的霜雪浸染
在哈佛教授俱乐部的那个幽暗角落里
熠熠生辉

身上却似乎仍穿着你的小说主人公武男
那套有点破旧了的
打工后去上学的西服

你带我出来，眼里冒着三十多年前的
那种激动的光，去找哈佛书店
背侧拐角处的那家诗歌书店

然后是道别，我目送你消失在
波士顿地铁的入口处——
在多少年后，这竟又让我想起了
但丁《神曲》第一部的开端

2023.3.10

Into the Boston Subway, for Ha Jin

A headful of white hair, doubly dyed by frosts
of New England and China's Northeast
radiantly glows from a dim corner
of the Harvard Faculty Club

Dressed like Wu Nan,* a character
in your own novel, who wore an old sport coat to class
not having time to change after work

You led me out, with that eager look from thirty years ago
around the corner from the back of Harvard Bookstore
to a bookstore specializing in poetry
Then we spoke parting words; my eyes followed you
as you disappeared into the entrance of the Boston subway
Once again, after all those years, you reminded me
of the opening passages of Dante's Divine Comedy**

*[Note: Wu Nan is the name of the lead character in Ha Jin's novel, A Free
Life. The book tells of a former graduate student who becomes a restaurant owner
and raises a family in America. (trans.)]
**[Note: In the opening passage of Dante's Divine Comedy, the narrator meets
the poet Virgil, who becomes his guide and escorts him to explore the underworld.
(trans.)]

在轮渡上

在从史丹岛到曼哈顿的轮渡上
我们路过自由女神雕像

有人依在船舷栏杆边拍照
有人坐在靠椅上晒太阳

她仍高擎着青铜火炬
只是你已听不到那早年的呼唤

到了美国，如同莎士比亚笔下的金钱
"自由"也成了一个谜

它让半个小时的航程变得漫长
漫长得足以上演你的一生

它让你久久注视那几只追逐的海鸥
看在你的船尾究竟翻起了什么

2024.3.13

On a Ferry Ride

On the ferry from Staten Island to Manhattan
we pass by the Statue of Liberty

Some people lean on the railing taking photos
some sit on deck chairs basking in sunlight

She still holds her bronze torch high
but you no longer feel her breath as in past years

Once your reach America, "freedom" becomes a riddle
like the Bard's remark on rich men, who see vice in beggary*

The riddle prolongs that half-hour ferry trip
stretching it to an enactment of one's whole lifetime

It causes you to gaze at seagulls chasing each other
vying to be first to find what turns up in the boat's wake

March 2024

*[Note: Shakespeare wrote, "Whiles I am a beggar, I will rail and say there is
no sin but to be rich; and being rich, my virtue then shall be to say there is no vice
but beggary." (King John, Act.2, Scene 1) (trans.)]*

2024 年 4 月 8 日日全食

从墨西哥城到华盛顿到蒙特利尔
到我们生疼的眼瞳的北半球
今日北美日食之奇观
正如我曾读到的中国四川诗人哑石的一句诗：
"墓碑贴着地面飞。"

2024.4.8

Total Solar Eclipse, April 8, 2024

From Mexico City to Washington D.C. to Montreal, it's coming
to the aching pupils of the Northern Hemisphere
the amazing spectacle of the North American solar eclipse
It's like a line I read once by the Sichuan poet Ya Shi:
"a gravestone comes skimming along the ground"

April 8, 2024

李笑虹/ Li Xiaohong

美国纽约州立基础研究院细胞神经生物研究室主任。作品发表在海内外多种纸刊并被多本诗集收录。2019 年应邀举办了个人专场诗歌朗诵会。诗歌多次获奖。著有个人诗集《虹》《风的弧度》和《色彩之上》。

Li Xiaohong is the director of the Cellular Neurobiology Laboratory at the New York State Institute for Basic Research. Her works have been published in various poetry journals at home and abroad and included in many poetry collections. In 2019, she was invited to hold a personal poetry recitation. She has won many awards for her poetry. She is the author of personal poetry collections *Rainbow*, *Arc of the Wind* and *Beyond All Colors*.

野花

我这样不停地绽放
像收集阳光一样，收集你的每一次注目
你知道我有多拼

我不是谁摘下的那朵
我只是河边，墙角
或者一片不着边际的大地上
最微小的色彩。
或浓或淡
涂在你用憧憬一挥而就的春天

某天，我会在一夜之间
毫无挣扎地消失
但我不会让你看到我流泪的模样
我的伤痛
永远深藏在我鲜亮与绽放的背后

Wildflower

Such is the way I blossom ceaselessly
Like gathering sunlight, I gather your every gaze
You know how hard I try

I am not one of those blossoms that are readily picked
I am here, beside a stream, at the corner of a wall
a diminutive spot of color, perhaps pale
perhaps vivid, a springtime dabbing of color
that by wishfulness you try to dash off at one go

The day will come, I will disappear
overnight without the slightest struggle
but I won't let you see my tearful countenance
My painful wound is forever hidden
behind the bright color blooming

夕阳下

这种油然而生的美好
是因为它会用挑染的有温度的词
描述每一种生命
包括那些潦草的，孤寂的
黯然神伤的
甚至已经凋谢的

还因为那稍纵即逝的瞬间
它弯下腰来的样子
像母亲

Beneath the Setting Sun

This loveliness seems to creep up
by means of its batik-like pattern of warm words
used to describe every living thing
including the sketchy and solitary ones
those suffering wounds of the soul
or even those withered-away ones

precisely because the moments are so fleeting
the look of one who bows at the waist
gives a sense of motherliness

空白—自闭症日记

是雪搬空了时间
你从我三千分行的字里走失
堪比一场虚拟的白
那些吹弹可破的絮
难道不是我打开你的方式？

一面镜子碎成无数片
我能从每一片里找到你

夜色似曾相识
搂着一棵树的海市蜃楼
有人在那里拾起过星星的只言片语
叶子还在枝头打转
它比充满的希望轻一点

我知道，不是风
而是一片空白
在怂勇我从雪地上抓出一道
长长的印

Blankness—An Autistic Diary

It was the snow that emptied out time, and you
are no longer found in the words of my copious verse
comparable to a storm of virtual whiteness
that icy fluff which gives way to a mere puff or a flick—
wasn't it my way of coaxing you open?

A mirror has broken into countless pieces
I can find you in every one of them

As I wrap the mirage of a tree in my embrace
night's darkness seems of long acquaintance
someone once retrieved word-nuggets from stars there
A lingering leaf still twists on a branch tip
a tad lighter than the fullness of hope

I know, it isn't the wind
but a patch of blankness
that prompted me to claw in the snow
leaving those long marks

冰果/ Bing guo

《纽约一行》编委。作品散见于《创世纪》《香港文学》等刊物。多首作品收录于《纽约流光诗影》《喊》《继续狂奔在反省之路上》等合集。

Bing guo (Ice-Fruit) is a co-editor of *First Line New York*. Her works are scattered in publications such as *Genesis* and *Hong Kong Literature*. Many of her works are included in joint collections such as *New York Streaming Poems and Shadows, Shout* and *Keep Dashing Madly on the Road of Reflection*.

春 天

我怕听见爆竹声
怕那些急促的、连续的巨响
和在半空炸裂开的碎纸屑落地的声音
把睡得香沉的动物们惊醒

它们应该在春天自然地醒来
说不准哪天、哪个时辰
只要春天到了
它们自然地
就睁开了眼睛

Springtime

I fear the sound of firecrackers
I fear that long series of staccato blasts
And the sound of cardboard tubes splitting apart in mid-air
Which jolts all creatures out of their sweet slumber

In springtime they should wake up naturally
Once the spring season is here
The right day and hour will eventually come
In a perfectly natural way
They will open their eyes

错 误

我做错了事情
不恳求原谅

我准备在湖畔的林子里挖坑
把那些后悔的事儿
一件一件地坦白出来
每说一桩就埋一粒坚果

松鼠缺粮的时候再把它们挖出来
让我的错误
犯得有些许善良

2018.2.10

Mistakes

I have made mistakes
for which I'm not looking to be forgiven

In a clump of trees by a lake I'll dig a hole
One by one I'll admit my regrets
for each one I'll drop in a hard-shelled nut

Squirrels that run out of food can dig them up
So to some extent there will be good intentions
that will be linked to those mistakes I made.

Feb. 10, 2018

Oakland 冰川湖畔

草木从坚硬的泥地里冒出来时
沉默地挣扎着
颇像一缕执拗而温柔的心意

有的嫩芽儿
丧生于几场意外的风雪

剩下的，比较幸运
从枯枝败叶的缝隙
绿色如潺潺泉水
流淌出来

猝不及防地
淹没我的心

Beside a Glacial Lake in Oakland

When new growth thrusts itself upward
Striving to emerge from caked mud
It resembles a determined impulse of the heart

Some tender sprouts give up their lives
Beaten down by unexpected snowstorms

Those remaining, being a bit more lucky,
Find openings between decayed leaves
And appear like rivulets of green
That trickle out from a spring

Before I can get myself ready
My heart is already engulfed

陳銘華/ Chen Minghua

祖籍廣東番禺，1956 年生於越南嘉定，1979 年 9 月定居於美國洛杉磯。中學時期開始寫詩，1990 年 12 月偕詩友創辦《新大陸》詩雙月刊，任主編迄今。著有詩集《河傳》及散文詩集《天梯》等多種。

Chen Minghua, whose ancestors hail from Fanyu, Guangdong Province, was born Dec. 1956 in Gia Dinh, Vietnam. In Dec. 1990 he co-founded *New World Poetry Monthly* and has served as its editor-in-chief ever since. His published collections include *Biography of a River* (poems) and *Ladder to Heaven* (prose poems).

空 洞

雲蠕動，西牆蠕動布拉克牆蠕動哭牆蠕動，眼、耳、
口、鼻、頭、胸膛……一個比一個空空的洞，蠕動向
西南

一千年又一千年過去，牆上的洞仍然流著血流著淚
生長

2024.2.10

Hollow

Clouds are writhing; the West Wall is writhing; al-Buraq Wall is writhing; eyes, ears, mouth, nose, skull, chest cavity… each opening more vacuous than the last, as the wall goes wriggling towards the southwest

One millennium passes and then another; still the openings in the Wall gape wider, shedding blood and tears

Feb. 10, 2024

樹 魂

週末在車庫角落無意發現一大盒被禁錮的靈魂，由於一層塑膠薄膜的封控，11 x 8.5 寸的身段依然光滑亮麗！這一定是很久以前的舊愛，因為新歡 DOS 電腦出現後，我已完全遺忘了她們

如今她們靜默而哀怨地望著我，那麼不知所措的眼神仍在盼望，回到同伴聚集遊行的林蔭大道上，或許明年春醒還可以再抽枝發芽

2022.12.3

Tree Ghosts

Over the weekend in a corner of the garage I stumbled upon a trunkful of locked-up souls. Having been sealed up in a plastic sheet, their 11 x 8.5" bodies were still glossy! These must have been my old paramours, because I totally forgot them after my newly beloved DOS computer appeared.

Right now they are watching me silently and mournfully, their glances beseeching me so helplessly, that it takes me back to a road through forest shades, where my companions once gathered for an excursion. Maybe next spring new growth can still sprout from their branch tips.

Dec. 3, 2022

荒誕劇 10

櫻花時節，華盛頓的天空開滿了密件碎片，諸神透過龜
裂的隙縫窺視 —— 一群渴望能再度勃起的人們

2023.4.21

Absurdist Theater Piece 10

In cherry blossom season, shreds of secret documents bloom against the backdrop of D.C.'s sky, with dryads peering through the cracks between— the glances of people wishing to have an erection once again.

April 21, 2023

谢炯/ Joan Xie

律师，诗人，诗歌翻译家，出版有诗集《半世纪的旅途》（2015）、散文集《蓦然回首》（2016）、诗集《幸福是，突然找回这样一些东西》（2018 北岳文艺出版社）、翻译集《十三片叶子：中国当代优秀诗人选集》（2018 美国猫头鹰出版社）、随笔微小说集《随风而行》（2019 美国易文出版社）、翻译集《石雕与蝴蝶：胡弦中英双语诗集》（2020 中国青年出版社）、诗集《黑色赋》（2020 长江文艺出版社）、翻译集《墙上的字：保罗·奥斯特诗歌全集》（2021 花城出版社）。2017 年荣获首届德清莫干山国际诗歌节银奖，2020 年诗集《黑色赋》荣获华侨华人中山文学奖优秀作品奖。作品在海内外各文学杂志广为发表，并入选海内外多种选本。

Joan Xie is a lawyer and a prolific writer of poetry and essays, both in English and Chinese, as well as a poem translator. Xie's poetry and essay collections include *Half-Century Journey* (2015), *Looking Back* (2016), *Nothing Made Me Happier than Finding These Objects* (2018). In 2017, she received Second Prize at First Moganshan International Poetry Festival in China. Her poems in Chinese appeared in prestigious poetry magazines such as *Poetry Journal (Shikan)*, *The Yangtze River Poetry Journal* and *Peach Blossom Poetry* in China. Her poems in English and translations are published at *Exchanges Literature Journal*, *Lips* and *Poetry Sky* in the United States.

远走高飞

你是否也是那些微不足道的：苞，花瓣，种子
成千上万，组成一棵树？
你是否已经被告知
你不过为那棵树而存在
那么，如果你落下
你又能离树多远呢？
我现在坐在你们中间
正在积极地寻找一只饥饿到愿意
用翅膀和我交换的喜鹊

Going Far Away

Are you too among the insignificant:
all the buds, petals, and seeds
that taken together comprise a tree?
Have you also been informed
That you exist for the sake of that tree?
Well then, if you end up falling
How far from the tree can it take you?
Now I sit among all of you
Actively seeking a magpie hungry enough
To have an exchange of wings with me

俄国套娃

六岁那年
我病了
出院那天正逢中苏友好日

首长前来视察
送给每个小病人
一个俄国套娃

那天
天很蓝
湖水碧绿
成排的杨柳如旧戏台上婀娜的宫女
我躺在三轮车后的棉被中

路过长坡时，蹬车的父亲
用力地干咳几声
扭头看看我

我闭着眼睛假寐
却在棉被下偷偷地玩套娃
我打开一个又一个
每一个都披着鲜艳的中亚头巾
大而圆的好看眼睛
上翘的长长睫毛

图案相同
神情却有微妙的差异
我打开一个又一个

一个比一个小
一个比一个接近真核
可是最里面最小的那个
却是打不开的
摇一摇，咚咚作响
被封在最小的套娃中的是
更小的套娃吗？
到家了　父亲将我抱进屋

套娃被他忘记在那辆
从街道居委会借来的三轮车上
很多年过去了
我仍然在想
打不开的那个套娃中
封着的究竟是什么
枯萎的味道
不到四点
路灯就亮了
桥头的旗杆上静静地
飘着星条旗
风一吹
落叶乖巧地滚落道路两边
我走到残云下空旷的足球场
做贼一样摘下口罩
窒息久了
连枯萎的味道都是好闻的

Nesting Russian Dolls

The year I turned six
I was hospitalized for illness
My release was on China-Russia Friendship Day
The director came through the wards
and gave a present to each little patient
a set of nesting Russian dolls
The sky was very blue that day
the lake was aquamarine
Willows made a wispy line
like palace ladies on an opera stage
I lay in a quilt on a pedicab
as my father pedaled up a long slope
Letting out a few dry coughs
and turned to look at me

I dozed with lowered eyelids
but held the dolls under the quilt
opening them one by one
each wore a colorful babushka
their lovely eyes were big and round
their long-upturned eyebrows
identically penciled
gave them a look of surprise
I opened them one by one
getting down to the smaller ones
getting closer to the true core

but the smallest, inmost one
could not be opened
It gave a rattling sound when shaken
Could there be an even smaller doll
locked up within the inmost one?
Reaching home; Father carried me inside

The nesting dolls were left forgotten
In the back of the borrowed pedicab
many years have gone by
but I still wonder
what withered smell was locked inside
that doll that couldn't be opened
It is just before 4 o'clock
streetlights are turning on
The Stars and Stripes flap quietly
on the flagpole above the bridgehead
A gust of wind sends leaves tumbling
along either side of the road
I walk to a ballfield under ragged clouds
and furtively take off my mask
After being stifled for so long
even the smell of withering is fragrant

遇到一树野梨花

在泽西市波罗镇小邮局后面
遇到一树野梨花
半蹲在早已遗弃不用的绿色邮筒上
脸色煞白，眼神惶恐
仿佛刚从前世的封墓中偷跑出来
嗅一嗅
尚有阴间的消毒水气味
我问，来干嘛？
她被我问中要害，搔首，弄姿
无法逃避形而上的严刑逼供
这时，一辆福特突然转换方向
铁锈
嗤的冲进鼻翼
她趁机莞尔一笑，温柔地
亲吻我宿命线越来越短的掌心
街两旁，短樱花抓住雨脚
细雨绵绵密密

Coming upon a Wild Pear Tree in Bloom

Behind a little post office in Bayonne Township
I came upon a wild pear tree in bloom
hunched over a green, unused mailbox
Her countenance was pale, with an uneasy look
like a fugitive from last lifetime's grave
Inhaling a whiff, I smelled
disinfectant from the underworld
and asked, "Why are you here?"...
which touched her sore spot; she looked stumped
unable to evade my metaphysical interrogation
Just then a Ford pulled in and changed direction
our nostrils caught the smell of hot steel
She seized the moment to smile sweetly
and kiss the palm of my hand
on which my life-line is getting shorter
Along the street, dwarf cherries reached out to grab
at the trailing skirts of cloud in drizzling rain

达文/ Da Wen

廣東台山人。畢業於華南工學院和
UCLA。廣東「原流」現代詩集團成
員。現為洛杉磯「新大陸詩刊」編
委，洛杉磯華文作家會員。作品發表
於原流、一行、新大陸詩刊、作品、
詩神、秋水、世界日報、國際日報、
僑報，並被收入《悠悠秋水——秋水
20週年詩選》《世紀在漂泊——北美
華文新詩選》《百年詩選》《21世紀
世界華人詩歌精選》等多種選本。
創作經歷被收進《台港澳暨海外華文
新詩大辭典》。出版個人詩集《氣候窗》(1993)，《凡風港》
(1994)，《四方城》(1995，四人合集)。

Da Wen is from Taishan, Guangdong. Graduated from South China Institute of
Technology and UCLA. Member of the Guangdong YuanLiu modern poetry
group. He is currently an editorial board member of the New World Poetry
Journal in Los Angeles and a member of Chinese writers in Los Angeles. His
works have been published in *YuanLiu, Yixing, New World Poetry Magazine, Works,
Poetic God, Autumn Water, World Journal, International Daily, China Press,* and were
included in *Yuyou, Autumn Waters - Selected Poems for the 20th Anniversary of Autumn
Waters, The Century is Wandering - New Selected Chinese Poems in North America,
Centennial Poetry Selections, Selected Chinese Poems in the 21st Century World* and other
poetry anthologies. His creative experience was included in the *Dictionary of New
Chinese Poetry from Taiwan, Hong Kong, Macao and Overseas.* Published personal
poetry collections as *Climate Window* (1993), *Fanfeng Port* (1994), *Sifang City* (1995,a
collection of four people).

逐渐远去

不必需要讲入大海
才开始关注边际的定义

不必需要整个下午 用乏味的声音
梳理空气的影子

可以假设有群人
互相陌生 并排而坐

可以假设夕阳为背景
面对鸥鸟盘旋

并且逐渐远去
可以想象鲸沫

喷洒的瞬间
比黑暗的降临更加漫无边际

Getting Farther Away

You need not enter into the ocean
before you become concerned with boundaries

You need not drone on all afternoon
teasing out shadows of the air

You can assume there is a gathering of people
strangers to each other... seated in a row

You can assume a sunset as the background
for facing seagulls turning in a gyre

As they get farther away
you can imagine the spout of a whale

And that the instant of its exhalation
is more boundless than the fall of darkness

战争之马——电影物语

舌头们冲锋的时候
声音绽放在树巅上
奔跑的阳光把阴影挑向天空

铁蹄敲着收割的节奏
当机枪的和弦漫过山谷
飞得最高的翅膀碎得最细腻

环伺的玫瑰中
他把马刀投向地面　像他的部属
更早的时候把躯体砌进浮雕

WAR HORSE— The Film that Told Its Story

At a time when tongues led a charge at the enemy
voices bloomed in treetops…
Racing sunlight flung shadows into the sky

Horseshoes were drumming the beat of a harvest
as the chord of machine gun fire swelled in a valley
The loftiest wingbeats crashed with the utmost fragility

Amidst onlooking roses
a man threw down his saber, just as his underlings
gave their bodies to be figures in a bas relief tableau

风 车

昼夜里我们是自在的景致
在森林平坦的床上
我们比人类活得更加不动声色

你们所谓的辽阔
是对颜色失掉敏感
用书本把疆界设立得无比雅致

唐吉诃德
我们无需相赴无聊的约会
放弃你与生俱来的长矛吧

在白云苍狗的队列外面
把难以舍弃的梦幻朝天竖起
学会在殉难中旋转　学会沐浴风

Windmill

Night and day we are a spectacle, content unto ourselves
On a smooth bed laid out in a grove of trees
Our lives are more nonchalant than any human's

What you call spaciousness
Is your loss of sensitivity toward a countenance
You use books to set up prim and proper frontiers

Don Quixote, there is no need
For us to proceed towards a humdrum rendezvous
Put down your congenital lance!

Beyond the troupe of white shaggy-dog clouds
Set erect your hard-to-relinquish fantasies
Learn to whirl in martydom for a cause… to bathe in wind

张耳/ Zhang Er

北京人，在美国东西两岸生活了多年，是多部诗集的作者，包括近年台北秀威出版的《海跳起，子弹婉转》，美国西风出版社（Zephyr Press）的 First Mountain（第一山）。张耳也从事海外诗刊和诗选集编辑，中英诗翻译。她翻译的美国诗人约翰·阿什伯瑞的作品曾在《一行》《今天》《诗歌岛》《当代国际诗坛》和《世界文学》上发表。她和美国作曲家合作的英文歌剧 Moon in the Mirror（镜之月）、Fiery Jade: Cai Yan（熠熠蔡琰）及 Tacoma Method（塔科马方法）近年在美国上演。

Zhang Er, a native of Beijing, has lived on both sides of the United States for many years. She is the author of many collections of poetry, including The Sea Jumps, Bullets Tactfully published by Taipei Xiuwei in recent years, and First Mountain by Zephyr Press in the United States.. Zhang Er is also engaged in editing overseas poetry magazines and poetry anthologies, and translating Chinese and English poetry. The works of American poet John Ashbery she translated have been published in *First Line, Today, Poetry Island, Contemporary International Poetry* and *World Literature*. Her English operas *Moon in the Mirror, Fiery Jade: Cai Yan* and *Tacoma Method*, which she collaborated with American composers, have been performed in the United States in recent years.

无的四季歌

民事刑事公共权益程序正义
如一枝新绿吐芽，佩桃花重点
自由的日影，若短若长

管他呢，汗与泪的区别
透雨过后一切重来。血
即使没有指纹，也同样流出冤情

天的概念在晴朗的秋风里
出墙，舆情与城管刷脸
通篇像枯黄的杨树叶翻飞稀里哗啦

不是口粮更不是招牌
不是你不是我也不是他的柴禾
水结成冰，泰山乎？鸿毛乎？被执行乎？

Song of the Four Seasons of Nothingness

Procedural justice in the public interest, civil or criminal
like a sprig of new greenery, the key points marked by peach
blossoms
freedom's sundial shadow, variably short and long

Who cares? As for the distinction of blood and sweat
after soaking rain passes, all must be redone. Although blood
has no fingerprints, injustice trickles out just the same

In a cloudless fall wind, the idea of heaven
peeks over a wall; public opinion and para-police do face scans
Yellow poplar leaves rustle to the last page, topsy-turvy

Not a portion of grain, not a billboard
Not for you, not for me, not firewood for him
Water freezes to ice: is it mountainous or feather-like? Was it
enforced?

事的四季歌

岸上的青草，明天的青草，
细雨毛茸茸，而生在心坎的草
锄也锄不尽，萧红说。

出水的就要面对，茁壮而简直
搅拌遗忘的深浅和幸福感
易碎的沉积。只有风追问，莲叶何田田？

算账和收获关于过去也关于未来
这时候这里写下的一行挑剔这里这时候
躲在葡萄架下品尝白云的无为。

看不透这场肥皂剧，猜不出党魁心计
避不开河边污泥，听不清录像里村长在说什么
只觉得经济不是泡沫，百姓不是，雪也不是。

Song of the Four Seasons of Events

Green grass on a stream bank, green grass of tomorrow
Velvety drizzle and sprouts from the bottom of the heart
However you hoe it, you can't hoe it all, said Xiao Hong

Release of fluid needs to be dealt with, thriving and forthright;
Mixing profundity with blessedness of forgetting
Crumbling of sediment; only wind wonders at veins of lotus
leaves

Settle accounts and reap the relevance of past and future
The line written at this time picks apart this very time
Hide in a grape arbor and savor the non-doing of clouds

Can't follow this soap opera or guess the party boss' plots
Can't avoid river muck or hear the headman's words in a video
I feel the economy is no bubble; neither are citizens, or snow

有羞就倒在街头

上帝倒在八月的街头
滚下台阶，膝前一只空碗
再喝两瓶就不再记得，自己
已经有七十八亿孩子，其中八亿
正在饥饿，一万万染病，却又怀上
一只空碗，里面放什么合适？

赶快赶快，不然长不大了
也长不好，预防针没用，空流汗
这棵遮阳树不结枣。谎花的说法
他们当然知道。您倒在街头
一样睡得好吗？黄粱梦里
云是面白的，还是肉红？我们现在

讨论伦理还是神学？问题沉重
如山，好比有了空碗，就会有人
敲着边鼓在街畔打锣。运足底气
惊动天堂塌下来，沉入海底。喝吧
碗喝高了自己
把您比下去，饿得心慌

When Ashamed, Fall down on the Street

God falls down on the street in August
rolls down some steps, an empty bowl at his knee
Two more bottles and He won't remember, He himself
already has 7.8 billion kids, and 800 million of them
are starving; umpteen millions are sick, with more on the way
So what would be fitting to fill that empty bowl?

Hurry hurry, or else they can't grow up
and won't grow well; vaccines won't take, just make them sweat
Shade trees here don't yield dates. All that empty, fancy talk
they know all about it. When you are supine on the street
can you sleep anyway? In the space of a dream, worlds can fall
Are the clouds white like flour or red like meat? Is it time now

to discuss ethics or theology? The problems bear down heavily
like mountains. So much that those who find an empty bowl
will pound drums and gongs on the street. The startled sky
will fall by the power of their breath, and sink in the sea
So down the hatch... the bowl has gotten itself drunk
and won't let you count for much... in a panic of hunger

岛子/ Dao Zi

出生于 1957 年。本名王敏，曾任四
川美术学院教授、清华大学美术学院
教授。诗人、画家、艺术批评家。
1997 年获得美国 HUMAN RICHTS
WATCH Hellman /Hammett grant 诗歌
奖；2014年获德国米苏尔社会发展基
金会 MISEREOR HUNGERTUCH
2015/2016 艺术创作奖；2016 年获韩
国美术协会 KOREAN FINE ARTS
ASSOCIATION [KFAA] 艺术功劳
奖，；2021 年纽约艺术博览会优秀艺
术作品奖。著有《岛子实验诗选》
《岛子诗选》及艺术史论著作十余
部。在国内国际举办个人绘画展20余场。现生活、创作在北京与纽
约。

Dao Zi, born in 1957. His real name is Wang Min. He was a professor at the
Sichuan Academy of Fine Arts and the Academy of Fine Arts at Tsinghua
University. He is a poet, painter and art critic. In 1997, he won the HUMAN
RICHTS WATCH Hellman/Hammett grant poetry award in the United States;
in 2014, he won the MISEREOR HUNGERTUCH 2015/2016 Art Creation
Award from the German Miser Social Development Foundation; in 2016, he
won the KOREAN FINE ARTS ASSOCIATION [KFAA] artistic merit Award;
won the New York Art Fair Outstanding Art Work Award in 2021. He is the
author of *Selected Experimental Poems of Daozi*, *Selected Poems of Daozi* and more than
ten books on art history; he has held more than 20 personal painting exhibitions
at home and abroad. Currently lives and creates in Beijing and New York.

暗 蚀

羽翅，朝向
透明窗扉扑击

地缘学的鸟类
遗传学的竹笼

门前，半亩血田
后院，一群裸猿

星河，静止
孤烟，更静止

透明窗扉，朝向
羽翅扑击

血田，无辜
羽翅，更无辜

不能无辜，却都
不得不无辜

羽翅，朝向
透明窗扉扑击

在焊死的铁闸门背后
万顷白纸汹涌

Hidden Corrosion

Feathered appendages hurtle themselves
Towards a transparent window

An avian creature according to geography
A bamboo cage according to genetics

Before the gate... a half acre of bloody field
In the rear courtyard... a troop of hairless apes

River of stars, in quietude
Column of smoke, even quieter

The transparent window hurtles itself
Towards feathered appendages

A bloody field...is guiltless
Feathered appendages... even more guiltless

Feathered appendages hurtle themselves
Towards a transparent window

Behind a welded-shut iron grate
An expanse of white paper is surging

圣 像

你为何要画袍？为了
不可见的罪罚——

我看见我的黑暗火焰熊熊
焦糊纸背，跃出
一匹剖腹白马

——未被邀请的同路人

蓝骑士睡去
夜与雾争执

Sacred Image

Why do you want to paint it?
because of crimes not seen—

I have seen my flames of darkness blazing
charring paper from behind, from which leaps
an eviscerated white horse

—Fellow traveler not yet invited

The blue-armored knight has fallen asleep
The night wrestles with mist

七重斜塔

一

那个词没等说出，双膝就跪进嘴里
杀手伏在对岸，从瞄准镜暴跳起来
雨栅栏繁殖，天使人质的倒影，繁殖

二

一群光头哲学家，静坐
老问题的矽谷，那个
定时的词埋在谷底，滴答作响

三

梧桐门框空空伫立，在金融遗址
一行老凤凰咣当启程，请
迁就光速，请拨回蚌珠磨尖的秒针

四

这么多粉红薄唇，集训
在口号高地。指令蛇的密语
绿化她们的细鳞

五

锥子剃头，斧头刺绣
一个大师，一世传授
旷野一声尖叫，决出花鸟生死

六

荆棘在燃烧，不—众生在枯焦
天穹沧桑，土地沁出砒霜
纵有天书避雷，徒然，在七级塔顶

七

链锯轰鸣，有些东西
金石无法剞成。人：一个错误的设计
尚未得救；尚未，从没落中升腾

Seven-Storey Leaning Tower

1

Even before that phrase is uttered, knees kneel down within the
mouth
a killer lurks on the other shore, enraged by what is in the
crosshairs
Trailing rain propagates, as do reflections of angels taken hostage

2

A group of bald-headed philosophers, sitting quietly
a Silicon Valley of knotty problems… and down at the bottom
they've buried that time-bomb of a phrase, ticking away.

3

A camphor-wood door frame gapes… at the former site of
finance
an old phoenix takes flight with clanking wingbeats; please
synchronize
with the speed of light, please dial back the pearl-tipped second
hand

4

So many thin-pressed pink lips, training en masse
on the high ground of slogans, and watchwords of the drill-
sargent snake
promote lush overlapping of their most delicate scales

5

A head shaved by a chisel, embroidery done by an ax
one true master per generation hands down such skills
a scream in the wasteland decides the fate of birds-and-flowers

6

A thornbush burns, separate sentient beings are charred
heaven arches over a diluvian epoch, the land oozes arsenic
Despite an arcane text, brought by lightning to a tower's tip

7

Amid a chainsaw's roar, some things cannot be shaped
in jade or gold: humankind, being flawed in design, has not
yet been saved; downfall has not yet led to ascension

文蓉/ Wen Rong

本名董蓉玲，文学爱好者。祖籍福建长乐，现居美国新泽西州。Cafe厨娘，爱工作像爱树木有力的躯干；爱写作像爱枝桠点缀的花叶。作品偶有刊登。

Wen Rong, whose real name is Dong Rongling, is a literature lover. Her ancestral home is Changle, Fujian, and she currently lives in New Jersey, USA. The cafe cook loves her work like the powerful trunk of a tree; she loves writing like the flowers and leaves adorning the branches. Her works are occasionally published in journals.

归

没有一种黑能把夜覆盖
就像我在夜的某处独坐，锅里熬着白粥
而我等候的人
他的车灯正把黑夜
捅出一个又一个光亮的窟窿

Return

There is no blackness sufficient to cover up the night
Not this dark spot where I sit alone, boiling a pot of white rice
Still there is someone I am waiting for
And he has headlights on his car
That poke two bright holes in the night

看"孤独"二字有感

在我的狭窄的屋子里
语言的帆迅速升起的时候真会遇上大麻烦
我需要隔着最少一片湖与你交谈
让帆船甩开的波涛经过岸边菖蒲草；
经过一只蓝鸟的歌声、和清晨未稀释的空气，
由它们布成的细网过滤后
轻而柔弱的落下几个，像晨光一样精致的文字
若狂风骤雨让我们不得不困在我
狭窄的屋子
我也不会轻易向你多走几步
距离的美只有那支落魄流亡的队伍见过
他们被种在历史深处，在绢布或泛黄的宣纸上，
隔着防弹玻璃开着幽兰
现在，我们之间因为天气的困顿
在我的狭窄的屋里，我们
刚刚开拓的湖泊、岸边摆放的石头、
还有种下的许多灌木
它们正缓慢地走向时间的磨坊
让整体再也无法分割

How I Feel When I See the Word "Loneliness"

In my cramped little room, I run into trouble
when the sail of language is raised too suddenly
We need to talk from a least a lake's breadth away
letting the boat's wake spread to bank-side sedge
through a bluebird's song, and dawn air's lingering freshness,
and having passed through their filter of gossamer fineness
to lightly let written words fall, as exquisite as morning light
If the fury of a wild storm should force us
to hole up in my cramped little room
I would not lightly tread the last few steps toward you
for the beauty of distance is best sensed among the ranks of exiles
those planted in history's deep places, on yellowed rice paper or
silk,
whose orchids bloom behind a plate of bullet-proof glass
Now between us two, driven to this plight by rough weather
here in this narrow little room, where the space of this lake
has been opened, by us, with the rocks placed along its shore
and plantings of shrubbery, all of them are slowly heading
towards time's millstone, in such a way
that the whole will never again be divided

曲未终

前半生，我用语言粉饰一切
现在好多了
当我站着，像乔木
转身像开花

An Unfinished Melody

In the first half of life, I prettified everything with language
Now is much better
Now that I am standing like a sturdy tree
simply turning about is like putting forth flowers

楚鸿/ Chu Hong

旅居纽约，在一家国际新闻
社任英文编辑。著有诗集
《年龄的独白》，并在多种
文学期刊发表作品，包括
《葡萄园诗刊》《两岸诗》
《香港文学》《纽约一行》
《新大陆诗刊》，MAYDAY 杂
志等。作品亦散见于北美、
亚洲地区的主要华文报刊。
诗作、散文入选海内外十多
部诗文集。

Chu Hong lives in New York and works as an English editor for an international
news agency. Member of PEN Chinese Writers Abroad Centre (CWAC) in New
York. She is the author of the poetry collection *Soliloquies of Age* and has published
works in various literary journals, including Vineyard Poetry Magazine, Cross-
Strait Poetry, Hong Kong Literature, First Line New York, New World Poetry
Magazine, MAYDAY Magazine. Her works have also been published in major
Chinese newspapers and periodicals in North America and Asia. Her poems and
proses have been selected into more than ten anthologies at home and abroad.

龙 年

捱……过
又　轮成熟的守候
丰收傲慢，在视野的焦点爽约
浮土借机遮掩了匍匐的心律
只能再压低一个音调：
结痂的希望
翻过时间的界碑
会重新长苗

烟花乐于试探雪与雪的亲密
悲喜剧都神往
冲散封锁后的眺望
传说中的神兽摆着头
调停了几千年机智的辩论
幸和不幸都
回到同一个原点

月光指引，划出等距的虚线
一次次努力拉平
愈发倾斜的起跑线
只有梦是知时节的：
煦风会意
把冻雨挡在了门槛外

2024 龙年除夕

Year of the Dragon

Having managed......to get through
another round of expectant readiness for ripening
the pride of harvest has not yet turned up in vision's circle
Airborne dust opportunely veils my crawling heart rate
All I can do is shift to a lower musical key:
As scabbed-over hopes
climb over time's boundary marker
they are likely to grow new sprouts

Fireworks gladly test if snow will gravitate to snow*
Tragic or comedic, after a blockade breakthrough
one invariably hankers for a distant view
In legends a wonder-beast turns its head this way and that
to arbitrate the thousand—year clash of nimble wits
Whether favorable or not
all return to the same origin point

Moonlight leads the way with equidistant dotted lines
leveling out various attempts
no matter how slanted the starting line
only dreams really know the proper season
The zephyr comes in an understanding way
blocking the freezing rain outside your threshold

*[Note: In Chinese, "snow" is sometimes used metaphorically to
mean redress of false slander or miscarried justice. (Tr.)]

On the eve of the 2024 Chinese New Year

失去季节的午后

喷雾机在屋角
哑摸水分了的细节，无言
模仿着人类争先恐后的唏嘘
明亮试图破窗而入
解救被困倦绑住手脚的清醒
而醒者无心解读
乱梦中潜伏的提示
不再想何处，何人
是否要在日历上多划个记号
似乎都不适合这样的午后
急救车的尖锐仍四处扎伤
耳朵或是心脏
这一次看得分明：
勒紧它喉头的绝望是
春天的背叛
时间到了，保护镜后
诡异的人类一一审视起
万物的忠诚
从心跳和口舌开始
从失去了季节的午后开始

2020 年 3 月，新冠疫情初期于纽约

An Unseasonable Afternoon

A sprayer in the corner of a room
raises wisps of water molecules into view, wordlessly
imitating the sighs of humans who strive to be first
Brightness barges in through a window
to dispel the paralyzed limbs of weariness
but the one who wakens has no wish to decode
the subliminal hints in chaotic dreams
no longer wondering which person or which place
Whether to add marks to a calendar is a question
that does not seem suited to such an afternoon
Ambulances on all sides make screams that pierce
both the ears and the heart
At this point it becomes clear
the despair that constricts the throat
is a betrayal of springtime
The time has come: from behind goggles
uncanny human eyes are starting to assess
the trustworthiness of other living things
beginning from one's heartbeat and manner of speech
beginning from an unseasonable afternoon

(March 2020, during Covid-19's initial phase in New York City)

秋的心脏里

色彩翻滚着
涌过来，夺去
我们的呼吸

光影摇曳，向着
缤纷搭起的隧道深处
梭行
天地永恒
赐予你我一刻的永生

现实在窗外
隔着一张玻璃，一把锤子
也许只是一个按钮的启动
你我却都没有动
任由目光虔诚
岚雾升荡

秋的心脏里盛满
季节的特权，伤感也是
我们伸臂划开的路
是天底向前的角度

2020.10.

In the Beating Heart of Autumn

A roiling tumult of colors
comes surging towards us
stealing away our breath

Light and shadow are tossing
around us who hurtle into depths
of a tunnel made out of profuse shades
Celestial and terrestrial eternity bestow
moments of enduring life on me and you

Reality is outside the window, and a hammer blow
may be no more than the activation of a button
You and I do not touch it,
allowing a gaze
to linger devotedly
and hillside mist to wreathe

The heart of fall has been poured full
of a season's bounty, as well as its blues
With sweeping arms we muscle our way
heading forward through the sky's bottom layer

October 2022

冷杉/ Fir Tree

青年诗人。出生于浙江台州，先后生活于杭州，苏州，马里兰州，密歇根州。浙江大学中国古代文学硕士，研究方向为先秦汉魏晋南北朝文学。做过记者，编辑，自由撰稿人。有中英文诗作见于中美文学刊物。出版有诗集《车前草》。

Fir Tree, young poet. Born in Taizhou, Zhejiang, she lived in Hangzhou, Suzhou, Maryland, and Michigan. Master's degree in classical Chinese literature from Zhejiang University. Her research direction is the literature of Pre-Qin, Han, Wei, Jin, Southern and Northern Dynasties. Worked as a reporter, editor, and freelance writer. Some of her Chinese and English poems have been published in Chinese and American literary journals, and she has published a collection of poems called *Plantain Herb*.

冷月亮

异乡人，这层层叠叠的夜宫
为你而铸，敌暗而我明。
你的孤独已成熟落地，无人捡食的
苦楝子：剥开它，挤压它，碾碎它
它的叫声并无侵略性，有
婴儿的甜梦为证。不要担忧，当他
重叩无痕的齿冢，紧攥手边的白窗纱
窗外一枚冷月亮。

往前走，别停下。河畔广场水晶宫
流光碎泄，黑巷子里有火舌嘶嘶
别停下。甩掉身后长长的白昼余骇
避开露台上，那个狙击睡意的年轻人
别停下。翻过天桥，穿越甬道
以芯片之蟒力，扭转翼闸之铁腕：
十，九，八，七，六，五，四……
城市的兽口就要关闭，众人收桨。看
中央公园灰枭群起，通讯塔尖
一枚冷月亮。

Cold Moon

Outlander, for you these storeyed night palaces were raised
dimness for the foe and light for us…
Your solitude falls like ripe fruit, no one picks it up
O bitter toosendan fruit: peel it, squeeze it, press it
Its cry is not invasive, as was proven by the sweet dreams
of a baby. Do not worry, someday he will pay respects
to a tooth buried in an unmarked grave,* and will clasp
a white curtain's edge where a window opens to a cold moon

Go without stopping. Beside the river is a plaza, a crystal manor
sending out streaks of light; tongues of flame hiss in a dark alley,
Don't stop, shake off the clinging daylight terror behind you
avoid the sharp-eyed sniper who waylays you with fatigue
Don't stop, pass over a pedestrian bridge, through a passageway
use the coiled force of a chip to turn back a relentless turnstile
Ten, nine, eight, seven, six, five, four…
The city's beast population is going to be closed off;
now everyone draws in their oars. Look, a flock of gray owls
flies up in Central Park; at the tip of a broadcasting tower
see the cold moon.

*Note: [1] In 1641, the army officer Li Kecong was sent on a campaign against
the rebel Li Zicheng, in hopes of protecting the last Ming emperor, Chongzhen.
The campaign was clearly hopeless, and the bodies of the dead would be difficult
to recover. Before setting out, Li Kecong yanked out a tooth, gave it to his wife,
and told her to place it in a grave where his son could someday pay respects to
him. In the story told of this event, the grave prepared for him was called a "tooth
grave." [Translator]

热病之城

我闻过它深沼般的气息。
我见过它埋首绝望的铁锈——
那些轰鸣一时又恒久死寂的机器。
我曾顺着它突兀的草莓舌
直抵盲肠之暗，
寻找一个盾形的出口——
那出口无比肮脏，
那出口，只有我知道。

会有一只夜莺在那里等我：
瘴疬无法染指的歌声
多么纯净。

暮色一样纯净。
钢铁之光
耸立在它的鸡皮疙瘩上。

在声道般向着外部弥散的广场，
那热病之城的核心，
享用你的晚餐——
注意面包里的铁钉，
敬重并拷问那面冷漠的墙：
为何大火烧毁了水晶宫？
为何一个名字破碎，
一个世纪紧跟着坠落泥尘？

烂尾巴别塔下睡满了乌合之众。
吃语仍在说着手可摘星辰。
福尔马林般的月光，
带着毁灭欲——
塑平坑坑洼洼的万物。

The Fevered City

I have smelled its swampy breath
and seen the rust of its immersion in despair—
those machines that roared awhile, then fell lastingly silent.
Once I went by way of its bulging strawberry tongue
to arrive at the darkness of its appendix
I searched for the shield shape at an exit—
that exit leading to utter filth,
an exit that I alone know.

A nightingale will await me there:
there is such purity in its notes of song
that the miasma cannot sully.

Purity akin to twilight.
With the glint of steel looming
on its horripilating hide.

On a plaza opening outward like a vocal tract
which is the very core of the fevered city,
partake of your dinner—
Beware of nails in your bread,
respect walls, but question their coldness:
Why did fire destroy those crystal lattice structures?
Why was a name smashed to pieces,
as a century toppled with it into caked dust?

Beneath a half-built Tower of Babel sleeps the rabble,
in dreams still raving that the stars here are low hanging fruit.
Moonlight pickled in preservative,
seemingly bent on destruction, casts a withering gaze
enough to flatten the lumpy mass of living things.

黑绳索

去往童年午后的道路：脑中
一条表面磨损的黑绳索，
像患重疾的咽部日渐纤细——
时间，它唯一的病种仍在侵袭。
沙沙作响的是记忆的雪花，
也是烈日灼着石榴树，
花的裙裾窸窣如蝉翼。

少年躺在路边，流云翻滚着视觉。
毫无快感的热洋流中，几千吨
乡村的虚无被点燃又抛高，
烟花般铺天盖地，那时时咬啮
夏天头盖骨的隐匿虫豸
开始了金属质地的尖叫；
那捆绑万物的黑绳索
打开并释放出粘稠的黑绒毛。

大地：绿色和金色汇成的挽歌，
它蟒蛇的母体，满布夹竹桃尸斑
旧日子般无人问津——
那些口渴，困倦，那些冗长书页
以一己之力捣毁的早熟肉体。
阴谋论的疾风弹折光束。
群鸭戏水的无聊感
即将攀爬至远山的尖顶。

此刻，作为童年的残篇
与那些随时自燃的图像坐一起：
"你做了一个属于别人的梦，
你未逢对手但一败涂地。"

Black Lasso

Heading down the road of a childhood afternoon
in my mind a lasso of black rope is worn smooth,
each day growing thinner, like an invalid's throat—
Time, its sole ailment, keeps closing in.
Memory is the hushed rustle of snowflakes,
but also a pomegranate tree under hot sun,
and flower-skirts make a "whish" like cicada wings.

Lying by a road in youth, drifting clouds churn one's vision.
Sultry thermal currents from the sea; massive tonnage
of empty village ennui, ignited and flung skywards,
pervading the air like fireworks, and teeth often clenched
from summer bugs on the scalp,
when they started their metallic whine.
The black lasso that bound all living things
opened to release the growth of thick black fuzz.

The good earth: a requiem that merges green and gold
python-like matrix studded with cadaver spots of oleander
many corners unfrequented, like bygone days—
All those thirsty, weary, superfluous book pages
and precocious flesh pounded down by one's own strength.
Urgent wind of conspiracy theory twanging beams of light.
Dullness of flocking ducks playing in the water,
about to mount to the height of faraway peaks.

At this moment, as a leftover page of childhood
sitting here with images that may combust at any moment:
"You were having a dream that belonged to other people,
even before facing an opponent, you were utterly defeated."

王键/ Wang Jian

1965 年出生于湖北省黄冈市，诗人。20 世纪 80 年代开始诗歌写作和发表作品，并成为武汉高校著名诗人。作品散见中外诗歌刊物，出版诗集《异乡人》《在回形针里跳舞》。自 2018 年起至今担任中南财经政法大学诗选集《山湖集》主编。现居纽约。

Wang Jian, born in Huanggang City, Hubei Province in 1965, is a poet. He began writing poetry and publishing works in the 1980s, and became a famous poet at universities in Wuhan. His works are scattered in Chinese and foreign poetry publications, and he has published poetry collections *Stranger* and *Dancing in Paperclips*. Since 2018, he has been the chief editor of the poetry anthology *Mountains and Lakes Collection* of Zhongnan University of Economics and Law. He now lives in New York.

在回形针里跳舞

回形针里别着上帝和舞者
它在弯曲里展开一部角力的戏剧
暴君和暴民，君子和黎民
生在同一时代。
针管上的舞者，用脚尖不断试探底线
在回字构成的云图里，他起舞
他向上伸展的双手，拉扯
星云的黑丝线
他试图拽下星云里的火柱
飞速旋转的双腿在平行线里移动
两个量子的纠缠画出迷宫般的逃亡路线
哦，我的主，我们拥有的是如此之多
请补上我们丰富的贫乏
请动手将自由的奴隶放出
并将那光中的裂隙用光填补
愿月光和汗水给舞者以胜过苦难的能力
他无力挣脱的负重，在地上旋转出
优雅而迷人的曲线
从起点回到起点，循环的故事像咒语
此刻，哈德逊河，像一枚大别针
正扼住曼哈顿的脖子
而在东方，黄河用九曲十弯缠绕大地的呻吟
我头顶星光，走向一台红色割草机
我要开动它，从日出到日落
让机器的轰鸣掀翻窒息的空气
让飞舞的刀片滚过杂草丛生的花园

Dancing in a Paper Clip*

Within a paper clip are clasped God and a dancer
In its curve unfolds a drama of contesting forces
tyrants and the mob, lordly persons and plebeians
all born in the same era. And a dancer on tip-toes
tests the bottom line of a syringe. In the cloud picture
of the character 迴 hui,* he begins to dance;
with arms reaching upwards, tugging at
the black line that runs through a nebula; he tries
to drag down a galaxy's pillar of fire
his whirling legs are circling in parallel
entangled quanta tracing a labyrinthine escape
O Lord, we possess so much:
please replenish our abundant poverty
please act to release the slaves of freedom
and fill in the cracks in light-rays with light. May moonlight
and sweat give the dancer strength over suffering
Let him spin across earth with his relentless burden
in graceful, enticing curves, from starting point
back to starting point, in a story cycle like a mantra
Right then, the Hudson River, like a big paper clip
is clasped at Manhattan's neck. and in the Orient
nine bends of the Yellow River entwine the good earth's moans
Starlight over my head descends on a red lawn mower
I want to get it running, from sunrise to sunset
let stifling air be roiled by that roaring machine
let the whirling blade roll over the garden's thick weeds

*[Note: The Chinese word for paper clip is 迴紋針 (huiwen-zhen), literally means
"needle that has a winding pattern." The word 回/ 迴 in ancient seal script looks
like a wisp of cloud. (Trans.)]

朝向寂静

在嘈杂、混乱、吵闹的世界
我，倾身丁寂静

我打开所有的器官
打开耳朵、眼睛、鼻子
打开手打开脚
甚至头发——
我朝向寂静

花开有时，落叶有意
万物演进的尺度
是在最小的单位
在看不见里完成——MO
朝向寂静

我靠近一首诗
靠近愤怒的词
但它却带着我像种子
在春天里飞行——
朝向寂静

我看见，长颈鹿将一个孩子送到树上
然后将头又埋进一桶水中
我听见，两个光年里的量子在对话
我观察和辨认一片地上的枫叶

如何飞向它的树梢——
朝向寂静

在四月，在乌克兰
在标枪导弹对准目标的瞬间
在弹簧刀无人机展开刀片的瞬间
在大威力的榴弹炮落下的瞬间
它们，都朝向同一个方向——

寂静！

Heading into Stillness

In the noisy, disordered, raucous world
I tilt towards the stillness

I turn on all my organs
I turn my ears, eyes and nose
turn my hands, turn my feet
even my hair—
in the direction of stillness

In a time of blooming flowers, a fallen leaf has a wish
The measure of evolution for all living things
takes place somewhere unseen
in the smallest increments
in the direction of stillness

I draw near to a poem
I draw near to a lyric of fury
and it carries me along
like a seed that goes airborne in spring
in the direction of stillness

I see a giraffe placing a child up in a tree
then its head plunges into a bucket of water
I see quanta having a dialogue over a span of two light years
I observe and see a maple leaf on the ground

and the flight it would take returning to a treetop
in the direction of stillness

In April, in Ukraine
a shoulder-fired missile locks onto its target
right when an artillery shell lands
both of them are headed in the same direction

towards stillness

一只等待出门的鞋子

带着雪，和
红海底的泥泞

带着一脸的疲惫
和憔悴

敞开胸怀，让汗
流尽，让光进来晒一晒

像阳光下的老兽
在睡眠中放慢呼吸

像回到子宫里的孩子
在蜷缩中，收缩
身上的皱褶

头，朝着大门口，即使
灰头土脸，也随时
准备好下一次的出发——

尽管它已走失了
那形影不离的另一半——

在流亡的路上！

A Shoe Waiting to Go Outside

It shows signs of exposure to snow, and to mud
from the bottom of the Red Sea

It shows weariness on its features
and a haggard look

Open its laced-up front to the air, let its sweat
flow freely, let light shine in to dry it
like an old creature in the sunlight
that slows its breathing when asleep

Like an infant returned to the womb
in a curled position that does away with
the wrinkles on its body

You are turned to face the front door, despite
your smudged and dusty visage, ready for
a new departure at any time

Though your other half that was beside you always
may have gone missing

Surely it too travels a wanderer's road

邱辛晔/ Qiu Xinye

出生于 1962 年。八十年代在复旦大学中文系就读后，任职上海三联书店。1990 年到纽约留学，之后在皇后图书馆工作。担任法拉盛图书馆副馆长近二十年。撰写、翻译、主编各类著作甚多。2018 年以来担任纽约法拉盛诗歌节执行委员；为《纽约一行》编委，纽约海外华文作家笔会副会长。

Qiu Xinye, born in 1962. After studying in the Chinese Department of Fudan University in the 1980s, he worked at Shanghai Sanlian Bookstore. In 1990, he went to New York to study and later worked at the Queens Library. He worked at the Flushing Library as a librarian and manager for nearly twenty-five years. He has written, translated and edited many books, including poetry anthology, biography, scholarly works, Chinese calligraphy and essays. Since 2018, he has served as the Executive Director of the Flushing Poetry Festival in New York. He serves as a co-editor of *First Line New York* and Vice President of PEN Chinese Writers Abroad Centre (CWAC) in New York.

生命的关键部位

女人的
乳房
鼓起了喂养两岸的浩浩长江
女人的子宫
垒起生命最初的安乐窝
而男人
运送精子的前列腺激流
堪比为摩西分合的红海巨浪

然而
生命关键部位的后戏
常常以扭曲与变异
掀起另一种潜伏的高潮
它在男女都不擅长编辑的
剧本之外

2024.3-4

The Crucial Parts of a Living Thing

The breasts of a woman
swell with the might of a great river
that bestows nourishment on either bank
The womb of a woman erects the walls
of the first cozy nest in a person's life
As for a man, the torrential sperm
delivered by his prostate is comparable
to the parting and meeting of Red Sea waters

And yet, the crucial parts of a living thing
often lead to a distorted, freakish denouement
stirring up a latent climax of a different kind
outside of the script instilled in men and women
where they cannot fathom what should be written

March-April, 2024

海

一片海是所有海的兄弟
但地球顽固着旋转的本性
于是
一波不服一波
浪与浪作战
在黑海
在阿拉伯海
在南海
在波罗的海
凌空三尺海浪尽情扫射

一朵接一朵
撞击成粉碎的
白色花朵
在惨烈的内战中
为曾经共享的低度和平
殉难

2023.4

Ocean

One expanse of ocean is the brother of all oceans
but the planet insists on maintaining its innate rotation
and so there is never a billow
that fully submits to another billow
Waves crash against other waves
in the Black Sea
the Arabian Sea
the South China Sea and the Baltic Sea
three meter waves overlook all the rest
wildly shooting spray from their tips

Crest after crest like white flowers
as they smash and break into spume
In this grim civil war they sacrifice themselves
for the sake of peaceful, low undulations
they once enjoyed in common

April 2023

品酒指南

封闭了一个多月
康乃馨只能在上海的内心
自我奔放
居委会说
再隐蔽也要献给白衣卫士
而我则读出了
刚入市的品酒指南：
2022 的白
酿出了 1966 的红醇

2022.5

A Guide to Wine Tasting

Having been sealed off for over a month
the carnation could only unleash itself
in Shanghai's inner life
The neighborhood associations said
no matter how hidden, it must be given up
to the guards in white suits, but my take on this
sees a key to tasting newly offered wines:
The white of 2022 will ferment into a vintage
that won't fall short of the red of 1966 *

*[The color white is associated with the hazmat suits of sanitation enforcers
during the Covid-19 pandemic. White was also associated with blank signs that
demonstrators held up during street marches against compulsory lockdowns in
some Chinese cities during 2022. (Tr.)]

May 2022

严力/ Yan Li

诗人、艺术家，1954 年生于北京。1973 年开始诗歌创作，1979 年开始绘画创作。是 1979 年北京先锋艺术团体"星星画会"和文学团体"今天"的成员。1984 年在上海人民公园展览厅举办了国内最早的先锋艺术的个人画展。1985 年从北京留学美国并于 1987 年在纽约创立"一行"诗刊（2000 年停刊），2019 年 6 月《一行》杂志在纽约复刊，继续任主编。2018 年出任纽约法拉盛诗歌节主任委员，同年出任纽约海外华文作家笔会会长。

Yan Li, poet and artist, was born in Beijing in 1954. He started writing poetry in 1973 and painting in 1979. He was a member of the Beijing avant-garde art group *Stars* and the literary group *Today* in 1979. In 1984, the earliest personal exhibition of avant-garde art in China was held in the Shanghai People's Park Exhibition Hall. In 1985, he came to study in the United States from Beijing and founded the *First Line* poetry magazine in New York in 1987 (it ceased publication in 2000). In June 2019, *First Line* resumed publication in New York. He continues to serve as editor-in-chief of *First Line New York*. In 2018, he served as the chairman of the New York Flushing Poetry Festival. In the same year, he became the president of the PEN Chinese Writers Abroad Centre (CWAC) in New York.

国 人

名叫"国人"的疾病
已治疗了千百年
但从今天起
所有的外科手术
都必须把病人身下
名叫国家的手术台切除
之后的治疗与护理
全部交由地球人管理

此通知来自外太空
国人没听懂
除了这首诗

2022.10

Countrymen

The ailment called "countrymen" has been
under treatment for thousands of years
but starting today
all surgical procedures will need to be utilized
to remove from the patients' bodies
that operating theater called "the nation"

This notification comes from outer space
My countrymen can't make out its meaning
except for in this poem

October 2022

飞

我一直喜欢仰望飞鸟
以及展翅的飞机
或者
滑翔的云

多年之后才顿悟
无论使用什么样的标准
风
才是飞翔的唯一高手
也只有风
在撞墙幢楼
撞山撞地之后
还能飞

2022.5

Flying

I've always liked to watch birds flying
also airplanes with their outstretched wings
or maybe clouds floating through the sky

After many years I finally realized
no matter what the criterion
only the wind can be called
the supreme master of flying
for only the wind, after colliding against buildings
against mountains and even the ground underfoot
it is still able to fly

May 2022

苦咖啡

阳光在上午八点后
弱弱地来到了我的窗台上
还能感觉到
阴霾慢慢地隐入大地的怀抱
我回味昨晚的梦
它分成隐隐约约的两部分
就像阴霾与阳光
我伸了个懒腰
端起那杯日常的苦咖啡
至于糖和奶
多年前就已被妈妈
存进了我的体内

2023.5.14.母亲节

Bitter Coffee

Weak rays of sunlight
come to my window at 8:00 a.m.
I can even sense
the haze retreating into the earth
I savor last night's dreams
which roughly belong to two kinds
just like the smog and the sunlight
I stretch my arms and roll my neck
raise a bitter morning coffee to my lips
As for the sugar and cream, they are in my body
already deposited there, over many years, by Mother

May 14, 2023 (Mother's Day)

www.ingramcontent.com/pod-product-compliance
Lightning Source LLC
Chambersburg PA
CBHW031521120626
46545CB00005B/1935